Sharing the Light

Celebrating the Second Half-Century
of the International Association of Torch Clubs

Publisher
The International Association of Torch Clubs, Inc.

Sharing the Light: Celebrating the Second Half-Century of the International Association of Torch Clubs

Copyright © The International Association of Torch Clubs, Inc.

https://www.torch.org

ISBN 9798321642146

Flesch Reading Ease index: 48
Flesch-Kincaid grade level: College

Disclaimer
Although the IATC, as publisher, and the editors and authors have made every effort to ensure that the information in this book was correct at press time and while this publication is designed to provide accurate information in regard to the past fifty years of the IATC, the publisher, editors, and the authors assume no responsibility for errors, inaccuracies, omissions, or any other inconsistencies herein and hereby disclaim any liability to any party for any loss, damage, or disruption caused by errors or omissions, whether such errors or omissions result from negligence, accident, or any other cause.

Credits
Photographs and images used herein that are not in the public domain are credited as indicated. The Torch logo on the back cover and anniversary banner on the front cover are registered International Association of Torch Clubs service marks. Front cover banner artwork courtesy of Outside the Cube Creative, Columbus, Ohio.

Contributors

The following dedicated International Association of Torch Clubs officers and members contributed their time and talents in producing *Sharing the Light: Celebrating the Second Half-Century of the International Association of Torch Clubs*

President
Susan Breen-Held, Des Moines, IA

Vice President
Arthur Bloom, Winston-Salem, NC

Centennial Project Committee Co-chairs
Douglas Punger, Winston-Salem, NC

John Tordiff, St. Catharines, Ontario, CA

Writers
Arthur Bloom, Winston-Salem, NC

Ann Weller Dahl, Westminster, MD

Arthur E. Goldschmidt Jr., Central, PA

Richard R. Lynch, Albany, NY

Douglas Punger, Winston-Salem, NC

Paul Scott Stanfield, Lincoln, NB

John Tordiff, St. Catharines, Ontario, CA

Joseph Zawicki, Buffalo, NY

Researchers
Chris Atzberger, Columbus, OH

Richard Davis, Columbus, OH

Raimund Goerler, Columbus, OH

Elaine Kruse, Lincoln, NB

Diane Selby, Columbus, OH

Stephen Toy, Delaware

Nancy Wardwell, Columbus, OH

Editing

Evan Thomas, Des Moines, IA

Liz Teufel, Des Moines, IA

Book Production and Formatting

Peter Michael, Frederick, MD

Susan Breen-Held, Des Moines, IA

Outside the Cube Creative, Columbus, OH

Joseph Zawicki, Buffalo, NY

Committee Secretary

John Vincenti, State College, PA

2023-2024 Board of Directors

President

Susan Breen-Held

Vice President

Arthur Bloom

Secretary

Dwight E. Williams

Treasurer

Paul Freiberg

Immediate Past President

Dorothy Driskell

Torch Foundation President

Pat Shutterly

Directors at Large

Tim Spaeder

Anne Sterling

Regional Directors

David Coward

Rod Gerwe

Ana Börger-Greco

Barbara Harrington

Steve Sosson

Gerald Stulc

Nancy Wardwell

Dwight Williams

Joseph Zawicki

Dedication

This work of many hands and minds is dedicated to the memory of

THOMAS L. CARROLL

Member, Winston-Salem Torch Club,

Founder and Member, Lincoln Torch Club,

IATC Executive Secretary,

and Torch's first historian.

Contents

===

A Letter from the IATC President

Since our founding in 1924, Torch has been an association of clubs with a single vision: to facilitate the meeting of professionals from diverse backgrounds to exchange ideas. This vision is still alive and strong in 2024.

Torch provides a place for those who are intellectually inclined—the curious, the life-long learners—to meet with people who may have nothing else in common beyond that core trait. And through Torch we are all enriched.

The organization has faced challenges and successes, and survived wars and a pandemic. We continue to adapt to changing conditions, using tools that are modern in our time to bridge distances and bring members from all of our clubs together for learning and fellowship.

In our centennial year, we should all celebrate the spirit of Torch. From our oldest surviving club in Fort Worth, Texas (1925) through our newest club in Williamsburg, Virginia (2023), our mission to bring people together for informed discussions continues to draw new recruits to us. The spirit of Torch has drawn families into the organization, continuing a legacy across generations in several clubs. And it has brought joy to individual members as they return for decades to continue learning.

I strongly believe that Torch people are all around us—they just don't know it yet. There is a spark of curiosity you will recognize in a kindred spirit. All of us owe those people the gift of bringing them into our Torch family.

To all of those who contributed to our Centennial History Project, I thank you on behalf of the organization. Your work is important. This volume will be interesting to the casual reader of our history, and an invaluable resource to our future leaders.

Sue

Sue Breen-Held, President (2022-2024)
International Association of Torch Clubs, Inc.
Central Iowa Torch Club

Donors to the Torch International Centennial Club

Founders Society ($5,000+)

Art & Mindy Bloom

Richard Lynch

Legacy Society ($1,000 – 4,999)

Sue Breen-Held

Ann Weller Dahl

Richard Davis: In honor of Art Bloom

Gary Hinzman: In honor of Dorothy Driskell

Gail Hoffman & Thomas Lane

Douglas Punger

Steven Sosson

Timothy Spaeder

Anne Sterling

Sandi Stewart: In honor of Art Bloom

Patron ($500 - $999)

Rod & Barbara Gerwe

Robert Schmidt

Pat & Michael Shutterly

Dona Wolf

Member ($100-$499)

John Bohmfalk & Barb Harrington

Nancy Carter

Dudley Chandler: In honor of and appreciation for Art Bloom

David Coward

Dorothy Driskell

Raimund Goerler

Arthur Goldschmidt

Ana Börger-Greco

Leo Kellogg: In honor of Richard Lynch & Anne Sterling

Ardyth Lohuis

Michael Mason

Peter Michael

Joel Stegall

Anne H. & David A. Thomas

John & Cyndi Vincenti

Nancy Wardwell

Dwight E. Williams

Marguerite Wilson

Joe & Ann Zawicki

Introduction: The First 50 Years

Written by Ann Weller Dahl and Douglas Punger

In 1991 Thomas Carroll wrote *The Story of Torch: The First Fifty Years of the International Association of Torch Clubs;* a pdf file is available at https://www.torch.org/uploads/1/2/4/9/124972626/thetorchstory_firstfiftyyears_thomascarroll.pdf. The following is a summary of this work.

1920s

Pretend with me for a moment that you are one of seventy-five men at the Radisson Hotel in Minneapolis on June 16, 1924. Your host, William F. Bullock, has invited you to learn about an international organization he wishes to form—a group whose members would be men from the professions. At this meeting he expresses his opinion that too often professionals tend to work and socialize with colleagues in their areas of expertise, so they do not really know what people pursuing other careers are doing. Bullock tells the group: "It has been my experience that professional men are so absorbed in their own fields that they really have little time or inclination to acquire an understanding of other fields. When circumstances require that attention be given to the views and problems of others, they lack appropriate sympathy or understanding...."

Just a month later, on July 10, 1924, the first club was organized in Minneapolis, quickly followed by others in St. Paul, Minnesota, Fort Worth, Texas, and Rochester, New York. By the end of 1929, thirty-six clubs had been chartered, many in Ohio, New York, and Michigan, some of which are still in existence today.

Very early in the process a constitution was drawn up, though Carroll's history of Torch notes that little in it would be recognizable to members of the association in the 1970s. Eventually, members from around the country were invited to serve on the International Association of Torch Clubs (IATC) Board.

Two curious facts about Bullock should be mentioned here: First, from Torch's inception, he wanted the word "International" in the title of the organization, even though it was thirteen years before the first Canadian club joined the group. Second, taking the title of Field Secretary, he drew up a ten-year contract for himself, subject to renewal, during which he was to be paid to organize clubs. For every member he recruited he was to receive $20. This is how he planned to make his living, and it was clear that he wanted little interference.

The Roaring Twenties chapter speaks to the establishment of Torch and the growth of clubs. During that decade there was a list of sixteen professions from which clubs could recruit men of good moral character and ethical standing. In 1927 Irving R. Templeton, an attorney, was named the first secretary of the IATC. He would serve over twenty years. In the same year the dues were increased from $2 to $3.

The history of Torch conventions during the first fifty years is documented in Carroll's history. The first annual convention was held in Buffalo in 1927, to which clubs were required to send a minimum number of representatives. The following year at the Columbus, Ohio, Convention the questions of "Who is a professional?" and "How can we attract younger members?" were raised, and not for the last time.

A publication titled *The Torchlight* was established in 1928, to which members could subscribe. This publication was later to simply become *The Torch*, which published outstanding papers written and delivered by club members at local club meetings. *The Torchlight* became a newsletter that is now emailed to all local club officers. Past editions of the magazine are posted on the Torch website at: https://www.torch.org/past-editions.html.

1930s

The Great Depression of the 1930s challenged the survival of many Torch clubs. Bullock resigned as Field Secretary in October 1931. In December 1933 the association's operating bank account had a balance of $3.77, but *The Torch* magazine as an organ for intellectual discourse was sustained. The first article written by a woman, Mary E. Woolsey, President of Mount Holyoke College, entitled "The Will to Peace," appeared in the April 1934 issue of the magazine. In 1935, due to the economic depression, a proposal was made to reduce the annual dues.

1940s

World War II dominated the country and the activity of Torch in the 1940s. No conventions were held in 1943, 1944, and 1945. The war also stifled efforts to celebrate the 20th Anniversary of Torch's founding in 1944. Conventions resumed in 1946 and club growth expanded, but the debate over qualifications for membership continued unabated. In 1947 two more professions were added to the prescribed list: actuaries and economists. The annual dues were raised to $4 per year at the 1947 Convention in Hamilton, Ontario. Sherman G. Crayton, Professor of Education at SUNY Buffalo, became secretary-treasurer-editor of Torch in July 1948, succeeding Irving R. Templeton, at a salary of $5,000 a year. His leadership would last for twenty years.

1950s

As described by Carroll, the 1950s began like the bright dawn of a new day. Thirty-nine clubs were chartered during this decade while fourteen dissolved, a net gain of twenty-five. In 1958 there were ninety active Torch clubs. An effort was made to form a club in London, England but without success. The debate over eligibility requirements continued. A proposal to allow women to be members of Torch surfaced in 1951 but was opposed by the board unanimously. After the US Supreme Court ruled in 1954 in *Brown v. Board of Education* that public school segregation by race was unconstitutional, the association affirmed that there was no bar to the admission of an African American to a Torch Club. By 1955, the eligibility list of professions had grown to twenty-five, but by the end of the decade Torch eliminated the list and gave each club the right to determine the professional qualifications of its members.

1960s

According to Carroll, the year 1960 marked the midpoint of the "Golden Age" of Torch, which began in the mid-fifties and extended into the mid-sixties. There were ninety-two active clubs in 1960. The one-hundredth club was chartered in 1961. Over the decade twenty-nine clubs were chartered and only three were lost, for a net gain of twenty-six. At the 1962 Toledo Convention the banquet speaker was a woman, Phyllis Grosshans, a political science professor from the University of Toledo, who spoke on international policy. Also at the convention, annual dues were raised from $4 to $5. The continuing concern about membership eligibility was expressed by Executive Secretary Sherman Crayton, who asserted that "we have a few members who are not truly professionals. This is unavoidable as long as we follow the policy of accepting anyone the local club has already accepted." During his tenure membership had grown from 3,000 to over 5,000 and the number of clubs from sixty to 115. In 1968 the net worth of the Association was $98,728.84. Crayton resigned in 1968. Robert (Bob) Nagel, an engineer and long-time Torch member from Knoxville, Tennessee, succeeded Crayton as secretary-treasurer. As the decade came to a close another proposal was made to amend the Torch Constitution to open membership to qualified women. Nagel, unlike Crayton who opposed the idea, wrote: "Societal attitudes are changing and Torch must change with them. The Association should no longer maintain a discriminating stand on the subject of sex within its membership." The proposal was postponed to a future convention.

1970s

As Torch began this decade, Secretary Nagel described the Association as "static." One club had not paid its dues since 1964; another since 1968. Membership stood at 5,333, the same as four years prior. Accurate membership records were not being kept. In June of 1970 Nagel informed the board that there was not enough money in the checking account to meet the payroll. There were substantial reserves, but no established policy on the use of them. In October 1970 the board granted Nagel permission to withdraw $10,000 from the reserves to cover operating expenses of the association. During the 1970 fiscal year the IATC had an operating loss but the interest on its investments was used to cover it. Proposals to amend the

Torch Constitution to allow the membership of women failed at the 1970 and 1972 Conventions.

At the San Antonio, Texas, Convention in 1973, IATC approved hiring a professional field service representative for the revitalization of weak clubs and the organization of new ones, to be financed by $30,000 from reserve funds for one year. For this position Torch selected A. Vernon Davis, Director of Development and Public Relations at Mount St. Mary's College and a past president of the Hagerstown, Maryland, Club. Dues were increased by $3. But the most significant action at the 1973 San Antonio Convention was approval of a proviso that any club that wished to could admit women, though the admission of women was not required of any club. Thus, the most divisive issue in the association's history was finally resolved.

In 1974 the number of clubs was down to 108, with several clubs seriously delinquent in payment of dues. Membership was down as well. The IATC's reserve funds had been reduced to $84,945.11. At an Executive Committee meeting in February 1974, Davis presented his "Torch Achievement Program," the theme of which was "Share the Light of Torch."

The Second 50 Years

As with any organization one hundred years old, changes in leadership and structure have created an institution somewhat different from that which Bullock proposed and then organized in 1924. But over generations the *raison d'être* has remained the same: the exchange of ideas among professionals.

Today there are about fifty clubs around the United States and one in Canada. This book will describe the significant events in the second fifty years of the International Association of Torch Clubs.

Chapter 1: July 1974-June 1984

Written by Arthur Goldschmidt
Researched by Raimund Goerler

Decade Overview

Although this history focuses on the International Association of Torch Clubs, its successes and failures largely depended on what was happening in the constituent local Torch Clubs. During this decade, the recruitment of new members and retention of current ones were key issues. Prior to this chapter's time period, the IATC Board had acknowledged that past volunteer efforts had failed to arrest the declining number of clubs and members since 1967. It formed a long-range planning committee, which met in April 1973, and recommended that the association appoint a paid field representative to advise Torch Clubs on how to recruit new members and to help form new clubs. This person's salary would be financed by raising the annual dues paid by each Torch Club member to the association from $7 to $10. This dues increase was rejected by the delegates to the 1973 Convention held in San Antonio. Instead, the delegates voted to withdraw funds from the association's reserves to pay for a Director of Development. The IATC Board chose A. Vernon Davis, president of the Hagerstown Club, for this position. Davis began work on February 1, 1974. He reported his efforts in "Briefings," an occasional newsletter addressed to club presidents and secretaries similar to *The Torchlight*.

The decade covered in this chapter saw some success in recruiting women to the clubs. Sophia U. Hedges of the Richmond Club was the first woman to attend an IATC convention as a member. In October 1974 *The Torch* magazine reported that there were thirty-one women members in eleven clubs and listed them by name and profession.

The period between 1974 and 1984 was marked by two economic and social trends that challenged Torch's ability to retain members and to attract new ones. The first was a general inflation of prices in the United States, due largely to the rapid increase in the cost of petroleum. Annual inflation increased from 11 percent in 1974 to 17.3 percent in 1979. Inflation increased the costs of producing *The Torch*, holding annual conventions, and meeting other expenses incurred by the clubs. In addition, inflation affected club members' discretionary spending, so those who were on fixed incomes found it more difficult to attend. The second trend, described in Robert Putnam's *Bowling Alone*, was a broad decline of membership in voluntary associations. Families headed by a professional person increasingly needed a second income to support their customary lifestyle. The professions were also becoming more competitive and consumed more time and energy. Television viewing, which had become ubiquitous in people's homes, was tempting during leisure hours. Clubs located in large cities or their suburbs struggled to schedule their meetings at times and in places that were manageable for professional people to attend. IATC membership figures must be viewed with caution, but our historian Thomas Carroll estimated that although 5,250 belonged to Torch in 1967, there were 3,581 members in 1984. The Association's net worth was $104,077.55 at the end of 1973, but had fallen to $6,172.54 by May 1984. In spite of all these problems, Torch International persisted though the decade.

July 1974-June 1975

In this year the leadership included President Leo G. Glasser (engineer), Vice President Forrest M. Smith (physician), Past President Norman P. Crawford (educator), Secretary-Treasurer Robert H. Nagel (engineer), *The Torch* magazine Editor W. Norris Paxton (educator), Director of Development A. Vernon Davis (journalist), and Directors Eric J. Pope (engineer), Thomas L. Carroll (public relations), Richard L. Jewett (engineer), Douglas Knudson (educator), and Jesse Long (journalist/educator).

In 1975, hoping to attract more papers for *The Torch*, the board initiated the Paxton Award for the outstanding contribution to the magazine.

At an IATC Board meeting after the 1974 Convention, the new development director broached the idea of forming a Torch Foundation that could receive tax-exempt donations.

Writing in *The Torch*, the president worried about inflation's effect on membership; IATC was balancing its budget with savings. It must either increase dues or membership numbers; it chose the latter.

In 1975 Glasser remarked that IATC had studied and restudied its problems. "Norris Paxton, a former president and now editor ... summed up the situation: 'If Torch dies, it will have been talked to death by those who love it most.' I decided when I became president to break some eggs and make the omelet."

Mini-conventions or regional meetings were held in Durham, North Carolina, on March 22, with five Canadian clubs on April 5, several Region 2 clubs in Allentown, Pennsylvania on April 19, and the southern California clubs at Laguna Hills on June 5, 1975.

The IATC office put out directives on recruitment of new members, a sample recruiting letter, news releases for local media, and plans for the development director to visit clubs. In June 1974 the IATC secretary reported 108 clubs, including new ones in Wheeling, West Virginia, and Laguna Hills, California. Torch had lost clubs in Denver, Colorado, Stanislaus County, California, Fort Lauderdale, Florida, and Charlotte, North Carolina. There were 4,896 members, a decline of 106 from the previous year. In response to the declining number of clubs and members, Davis announced his Torch Advancement Program in 1974, hoping to attract five hundred new members in 1975. The program's main elements were (1) membership development, (2) public relations, and (3) revising the organizational format to restate the case for Torch in more contemporary terms. He planned to write a letter to each existing club, giving specific membership goals and training directives on recruitment, program development, and improving the papers submitted to *The Torch*. The development director planned to "live with" each top-priority new club, working with the relevant regional director. New clubs were chartered in Boca Raton, Florida, on April 14, Stroudsburg, Pennsylvania, on June 10, and Pinellas, Florida, on June 17. By the 1975 Convention there were 108 clubs and 4,673 members.

The 1975 Convention met in Orlando, Florida, June 22-25. It attracted 178 delegates from fifty-one clubs, and ninety-two non-members attended. No theme was stated in the program and no keynote speaker was announced.

The President's Award went to the Athens, Georgia, Club; the Albany and San Antonio Clubs were runners-up. (This designation resolved what would have been a three-way tie.)

The convention approved the 1975 budget, which projected a $20,675 deficit. Much of this was due to hiring Davis as Director of Development. Paxton announced his retirement as editor of *The Torch*. Succeeding him in July was Lee Hoffman, who had been Associate Editor since 1971.

Entertainment included a Polynesian luau at Disney World and trips to Sea World and the Kennedy Space Center. Members were urged to spend time at Disney World after the convention, and the hotel extended its special member rates for two additional nights. In *My Life in Torch,* Carroll describes the Orlando Convention as a "near disaster" but does not explain why. He writes that the host club was dissolved soon after the convention.

July 1975-June 1976

In 1975-1976 the leadership included President Harry J. Krusz (also Torch Foundation president), President Elect Forrest M. Smith, Jr. (physician), Vice President Arthur I. Palmer, Jr. (lawyer), Secretary-Treasurer Robert H. Nagel (engineer), Editor Lee Hoffman (journalist), Director of Development A. Vernon Davis (journalist), Past President Norman P. Crawford (educator), and Directors Eric J. Pope (engineer), Thomas L. Carroll (public relations), Arthur Palmer (lawyer), Richard L. Jewett (engineer), Douglas M. Knudson (educator), and Jesse R. Long (journalist/educator).

At this time the IATC's central office was located on the campus of the University of Tennessee at Knoxville. Since 1968 it had shared space with the Tau Beta Pi Association (an engineering honor society). Secretary-Treasurer Nagel and a staff of three secretaries served both organizations. The secretary-treasurer was the one officer who received a salary from the association, for he did most of the work. In June 1976 Nagel resigned due to poor health, raising a challenge for the IATC, although its central office still was in Knoxville.

Writing in *The Torch*, President Krusz observed that the rising generation of community leaders was less likely to join organizations than previous generations, but he added that Torch Clubs offer opportunities for intellectual pursuit without large-scale committee involvement. He wrote, "Show them what Torch offers."

In July Davis reported on progress toward his goal of five hundred additional members in 1975. This included members of the new club at Boca Raton, Florida, chartered in April 1975. Davis visited the Minneapolis and St. Paul Clubs, as well as the incipient Rochester, Minnesota, Club. He also reported to the board on nine possible new clubs. However, in January 1976, the board voted to end his position, effective April 1, after two years on the job. His salary had cost the IATC $60,000 with disappointing results. The board decided to charge the ten regional directors with the task of developing new clubs and attracting new members, a policy that it called "regionalism." The Michiana (Michigan and Indiana) Club was chartered in June 1976. At year's end there were 108 clubs and 4,673 members.

The 1976 Convention was held in Columbus, Ohio, June 23-26. Its theme was "'76 and Beyond." One hundred forty members attended, representing fifty-eight clubs. Total attendance was 235.

John Glenn spoke on "Can We Govern for the Future?" The President's Award was presented to the San Antonio Club.

Convention participants completed a questionnaire, showing much interest in the processes and strategies for strengthening clubs. They liked workshops and expressed interest in having IATC provide some financial support for delegates to attend meetings. The convention had fewer programs than in previous years, but gave more attention to club organization, development, and procedures. The Torch Logo was redesigned and approved by the board in June 1976. The redesign was discussed in *The Torch* (July 1976) and the new logo was on the cover of the October issue.

Convention tours included the German Village, Battelle Memorial Institute, and the Ohio Historical Center.

July 1976-June 1977

Leadership included President Forrest M. Smith, Jr. (physician), President Elect Arthur I. Palmer, Jr. (lawyer), Vice President Douglas M. Knudson (forestry educator), Immediate Past President Harry J. Krusz (retired), Editor Lee Hoffman (journalist), Secretary-Treasurer Thomas L. Carroll (public relations), Directors N.P. Crawford (educator), John B. Dowler (engineer), Jesse R. Long (journalist-educator), Clifton E. Rodgers (landscape architect), Fred R. Whaley, Jr. (administrator), and Elsworth F. Woods (educator).

Nagel resigned as secretary-treasurer, posing a challenge for the association, which briefly kept its office in Knoxville. In the fall, Carroll volunteered to serve as secretary-treasurer. The central office moved to Lincoln, where he worked as Executive Director of the Safety Council of Nebraska. Carroll surveyed club practices and actively produced publications and reports. These included a *Manual of Administrative Procedures*, new versions of "Introducing Torch," "A Better Torch Paper," "A Handbook on Membership Development and Recruitment," and a yearbook. The board authorized sending *The Torch* to public libraries in areas where Torch clubs were located. It authorized the production of a quarterly, low-cost newsletter for club officers called *The Torchlight*, which Carroll started in March.

What does "Torch Club" mean to you? Is it a broadening experience, mental stimulation, enjoyable evening with friends? Is it a chance to match wits with peers, sample the opinions of people from other professions and generations, define problems of the community and the world? Is it an opportunity to offer guidance, friendship and understanding without thought of return? Torch means different things to different people. But it can mean all of these.

I often adapt a quote from Lord Rayleigh to say, "When you understand a situation well enough to define the basic problem, then you can begin to do something about it." Torch Club provides the forum wherein is developed the understanding which enables members to define problems in their own terms.

Discussions with members and discussion of papers help members to clarify their thinking and to formulate plans for their own activities. With this preparation they can better fulfill their roles in their vocations, churches, schools, community agencies, professional associations and other areas of society where they have responsibilities. And they can proceed with assurance, knowing they are working with reasoned approaches on the right problem.

Membership in Torch offers even more. Torch differs from other discussion clubs, such as town-and-gown groups, and the difference is very significant. The club is just the tip of the iceberg-the first in a series of wider horizons. The club is composed of people all from the same community. The next horizon reveals regional activities of Torch members from nearby communities and neighboring states. Still wider horizons open up in Association affairs-the annual convention, Torch magazine and Association committees. Although Torch clubs are the prime focus, regional activities and Association functions afford additional opportunities for communication and understanding.

Regional meetings bring together people from communities spanning hundreds of miles. A wider range of professions, cultures, ages, problems and viewpoints is represented.

Conventions and The Torch magazine bring together people and thoughts representative of

(Continued on page 4)

The story of our ambitious but vitally important Torch objectives for 1975 is reported on the news pages of this issue.

After my first year with Torch, in which we put into motion a number of activities involving public relations, future organizational format, restatement in contemporary terms of the Case for Torch, and membership development, we must this year concentrate on obtaining measurable results in membership development.

We must have a net growth of 850 members in this calendar year: 400 additional members in present clubs, and another 450 in 15 clubs that must be organized in 1975.

Written association programs, such as the one I have prepared this year for Torch, must be more than subjects for proper placement in administrative file cabinets. They must be generally known about and understood by all members, and enjoy the full support and "spiritual commitment" of leadership at all levels.

My 1975 development program, calling for 850 new members, is built upon these foundation stones:

1. An ambitious new-member recruitment program within existing clubs, with specific goals for each club, and communication regarding these goals reaching every member of Torch.

2. A new and consistent program of publishing training and guidance materials for use by club leaders, including "how to" suggestions regarding membership recruitment, making program building, etc., use of successful experience from clubs throughout the association.

3. The Director of Development will, within the limitations of time and budget, "live with" each top-priority new-club project, and keep the pertinent regional directors informed of developments so that they can play stronger supportive roles in the chartering process.

4.There will be continued visitations by the Director of Development to clubs throughout the country, with emphasis on those clubs seeking guidance on membership and program development.

5. We will strengthen the service-to-local-clubs aspects of association activity, including expansion of the service aspects of Briefing, the monthly newsletter

Leo Glasser and A. Vernon Davis, *The Torch*, April 1975

In May 1977 the executive committee, acting on Carroll's advice, hired Dennis Garrett as Director of Club Services. A recent graduate of the University of Nebraska, Garrett had majored in communication. His tasks were to expand and develop clubs and to write a new directors' manual. He reported to Carroll, who later wrote that he hoped the young man would eventually succeed him as executive secretary.

In 1976-1977 the board made significant decisions. It appointed a special committee, which met in November to draft an action plan for creating new clubs and a set of procedures to rescue weak clubs and encourage strong ones. It proposed holding regional "mini-conferences" to develop leadership. The board granted $250 each to Regions 3 and 5 for regional mini-conventions. These conventions attracted 170 attendees. The committee also granted $250 to Region 10 to conduct a regional convention in fall 1977. The IATC Board policy of regionalism put heavy responsibilities on the regional directors. Carroll was asked to write a list of the services provided by the association, since clubs often asked: "What does IATC do for us?" The board authorized Carroll to charter the Rockingham, Virginia, and Connecticut Shoreline Clubs, even though they had insufficient members. The latter club was chartered in January 1977.

In its January 1977 meeting the board of directors changed Carroll's title from Secretary-Treasurer to Executive Secretary. The board proposed revisions to the constitution and bylaws. The changes were reported in *The Torch* (April 1977) and were to be voted on at the July 1977 Convention. In *The Torch* President Smith stated that IATC's minimum goal was to form one new club in each region and to add two or three members to each existing club. He encouraged the clubs to send representatives to the 1977 Convention in Long Beach.

Between January and March the central office conducted a survey to find out how many clubs had women members. There were 119 women members reported in April 1977. The board considered raising the initiation fee from $7 to $10 and the annual fee from $10 to $20. In July 1977 the board proposed raising the member initiation free from $10 to $15.

The 1977 Convention met in Long Beach, California, on the *Queen Mary*, on July 12-15. Its theme was "Opening of a Western Vista." This was the first and only west coast Torch convention. Two clubs, Long Beach and Laguna Hills, hosted and 118 members attended, representing forty-seven clubs.

The first Paxton Lecture was given at this convention. Seymour A. Horwitz (physician) spoke on "Doctors' Problems for Laymen to Solve." The President's Award for 1976-77 was given to the Richmond, Virginia, Club.

The Long Beach Convention amended the IATC constitution and bylaws in several ways. The revised constitution provided for enrollment of individual members-at-large. This was to enable IATC membership outside of any local Torch Club. These individual members might later form new clubs. The revised bylaws eliminated "learned" from its description of the professions and eliminated "civic wellbeing" from its general purpose section; deleted the obligation of service as a criterion for membership; set twenty (instead of thirty) members as the minimum number for a new club to be chartered; raised the status of emeritus members, to be based solely on long or meritorious service; indemnified IATC employees on the same basis as officers and directors; spelled out central office assistance to regions and clubs; provided partial subsidization for regional conventions by a portion of dues; allowed funding of all IATC activities through an equitable and flexible dues structure; and raised the initiation fee from $7 to $10.

Entertainment featured concerts by the Long Beach Municipal Band, the Hollywood Bowl Symphony, and the Long Beach Symphony Orchestra.

July 1977-June 1978

Leadership included President Arthur I. Palmer, Jr. (lawyer), President Elect Douglas M. Knudson (forester), Vice President Clifton E. Rodgers (landscape architect), Past President Forrest M. Smith, Jr. (physician), *The Torch* Editor Lee Hoffman (journalist), Executive Secretary Thomas L. Carroll (organization management), Directors Fred R. Whaley, Jr., Everett H. Hopkins, Anthea C. Duron, Len Harbour, Richard M. Wolfe, Elsworth P. Woods, and Francis J. Flynn. Dennis E. Garrett became Director of Club Services as of June 1, 1977.

In June Carroll announced the following IATC publications: "Introducing Torch," "How to Organize a Torch Club," "Handbook on Membership Development and Recruitment," "Manual on Administrative Procedures" (the "Blue Book"), "Convention Administrative Manual," "Sample Torch Club Bylaws," and a *Yearbook* for 1977-1978 (the "Red Book"). He also wrote a revision of "A Good Torch Paper," which stipulated that the paper should have contemporary significance, universality of interest, freshness, substance, and a provocative thesis.

In August, Carroll noted with concern the falling attendance at conventions. Some board members considered reducing the number of days to reduce cost to their participants. A "Club Practices" survey was conducted in 1977-1978 by Carroll and Garrett, who issued their final report in May 1978.

Garrett met with the local officers of twenty-nine clubs. After having visited eighteen, he stated to the board in December that "most clubs do not know WHO the Association is, WHAT the Association does, or WHY we have an Association." Nevertheless, in spring 1978 Palmer noted in *The Torch* that, by hiring Garrett to improve club services and with Hoffman's continued success as *The Torch* editor, the organization seemed to be running smoothly. However, in June 1978 Garrett wrote a scathing report, arguing that most clubs were in a deteriorating condition, had poor policies and practices, poor papers, poor standards of admission, and apathetic officers. He noted clubs' poor relations with the IATC office. The clubs did not respond to seminars for development; they were too parochial. *The Torch* was weakened by its separation from the central office. Members knew that receiving it was a tangible symbol of what they paid dues for, but most did not read it. Existing clubs were not interested in creating new clubs because of the effort that it would require.

Garrett led an experimental series of leadership conferences, to which twenty-three clubs sent representatives, and two regional conferences. The IATC's first regional convention was held in Asheville, North Carolina, on September 30 and October 1. More than eighty attended.

Another regional convention took place on November 12 in Indianapolis for Region 10. Both mini-conventions stressed leadership training and club growth. One hundred seventy attended one or the other. The spring issue of *The Torch* reported that six leadership seminars had been held in the last three months. Their purpose was to provide the local clubs with reliable information on club practices and solving club problems.

Carroll reported a continuing decline in number of clubs, from 109 to 103, and in membership from 4,751 to 4,446. The Sonoma County, California, Club closed early in 1978. He also observed that regionalism as practiced thus far had failed to stem the decline. The At-Large membership category that had been introduced last year led to only three new members. As of December 31, 1977, Torch had 4,541 members, but as of June 1978 the number had fallen to 4,440.

The 1978 Convention met in Hershey, Pennsylvania, June 28-July 1. Its theme was "Regionalism in Operation" and sixty-one clubs were represented. Total attendance was 256. Maurice Goddard, Pennsylvania Secretary of Environmental Resources, spoke on resource management.

The Paxton Lecture was given by James E. Ingram, a lawyer and former professional football player with the Houston Oilers. Its title was "The History, Psychology and Philosophy of Violence in Competitive Sports." It had been delivered before the San Antonio Torch Club in January 1978. The President's Award was given to the Kalamazoo, Michigan, Club. President Knudson announced that the next convention would feature a new award: Most Improved Club. (The Muncie, Indiana Club would be later listed as having received the 1978 Most Improved Club award.)

At this convention there was significant discussion on the future of Torch. Carroll reported that the clubs' aging membership and enervated leadership were the main reasons for Torch's decline. He added: "There can be no progress if we continue to follow the theory that local clubs are entitled to go their own way, no matter how counter-productive that way may be." He argued that the IATC must adhere to the concept of regionalism that emphasized leadership. There must be an effective partnership between professional staff and volunteers. Knudson announced an initiative proposed by Thatcher Wood to recruit members under the age of forty-five.

Convention activities included visits to the Milton Hershey School and the Hershey Medical Center. Torch announced that it had arranged group tours to Guatemala, the Canadian Rockies, and the Caribbean in 1979. There is no evidence that they occurred.

At the board meeting following the convention Garrett announced his resignation to pursue an MBA degree and get married. His position as Director of Club Services was never filled again.

July 1978-June 1979

Leadership included President Douglas M. Knudson (forester), President Elect Clifton E. Rodgers (landscape architect), Vice President Fred R. Whaley, Jr. (administrator), Immediate Past President Arthur I. Palmer, Jr. (lawyer), *The Torch* Editor Lee Hoffman (journalist), Executive Secretary Thomas L. Carroll (organization manager), and Directors Everett H. Hopkins, Anthea C. Duron, Len Harbour, Arnoldus Goudsmit (later replaced by Paul Stanfield), Robert S. Rosow, Francis J. Flynn, and William A. Burian.

In its November 1978 meeting the board discontinued the post of Director of Chapter Services, approved the creation of the Torch Foundation, announced that *The Torchlight* would be sent to all club members, and announced optimistically that its 1979 budget would include $4,700 in additional receipts based on "an extraordinary increase in new members due to efforts of the Regional Directors."

The 1979 the "Red Book" reported 100 clubs in the USA and three in Canada.

The 1979 Convention met in Norfolk, Virginia, on June 17-20. Its theme was "Oceans." Total registration was 204, with 121 members representing fifty-three clubs.

The President's Award went to the Lincoln, Nebraska, Club.

Members offered proposals to amend the bylaws: enumerating categories of professions for membership while specifying that clubs should not have more than 20 percent in any one category, and removing the president elect from the board of directors.

Entertainment included tours of the Chrysler Museum, the U.S. Naval Base, and the Hermitage Foundation Museum, as well as a boat excursion around Hampton Roads.

July 1979-June 1980

Leadership included President Clifton E. Rodgers (landscape architect), Vice President Everett H. Hopkins (educator/administrator), Past President Douglas M. Knudson (forester), Editor Lee Hoffman (journalist), Executive Secretary Thomas L. Carroll (organization manager), and Directors Fred R. Whaley, Jr. (administrator), John M. Adams (engineer), Everett H. Hopkins (administrator/educator), Anthea Carol Duron (travel writer/lecturer), L.T.C. Harbour (clergyman), Clarence A. Peterson (investment portfolio manager), Paul Stanfield (editorial writer), Robert S. Rosow (CPA), Francis J. Flynn (university administrator), and William A. Burian (social work educator).

In the Fall 1979 issue of *The Torch* Past President Knudson commented that three recent developments had strengthened the organization: acceptance of women, renewal of regional meetings, and the creation of the Paxton Lectureship.

In March 1980 the board proposed to realign its regions with six directors instead of ten to cut costs. The realignment more nearly equalized the number of clubs in each region. In that same month the Executive Committee reduced the size of the board from twelve to ten and reported that membership remained at 4,285. It tabled a proposal to give free subscriptions of *The Torch* to public libraries in communities that had Torch clubs. It reported that in the last twelve months three new clubs were added and one lost. There was no success in adding new members under the age of thirty.

In its May meeting, the Executive Committee created an Editorial Board to review papers for publication in *The Torch*. Previously this had been done by the editor. In that meeting the board also created a category of "Honorary Lifetime Member."

In May 1980 Executive Secretary Carroll gave his final report. Among his publications was the "Reservoir of Leadership for Regional Directors," to assist their regions' clubs. He had conducted a study of defunct clubs to identify patterns of decline. He advised the board that clubs formed in the last ten years might need some IATC attention to assure development. He proposed to send *The Torchlight* to all members, not just club officers, each quarter.

Carroll reported an operating deficit of $3,061 in the 1979 calendar year. In May 1980 he noted that, at the end of December 1979, receipts had declined by $4,266. This deficit left a bank balance of $1,763. Its balance was saved by the arrival of early dues payments from some of the clubs. To address the shortfall in funds, the board decided to increase each club's dues by $5. In its May meeting the board also discussed creating an advisory committee of nationally known and distinguished people, but took no action.

The board decided to replace the departing Carroll by contracting with the Chicago-based Bostrom Management Corporation. The central office of Torch moved from Lincoln, Nebraska, where Carroll lived, to Chicago. It would be paid $30,600 annually for the following services: financial record keeping and statements, budget preparation, dues billing, promotion and retention of membership, preparing and distributing a newsletter, coordinating the production of publications, and maintaining membership records. David Lister of Bostrom would become the IATC Executive Director, effective July 1. He would also be the editor of *The Torch*. When Lee Hoffman retired, an editorial committee took charge of selecting articles for the magazine and Bostrom took over its production. For a short time, Lister was both executive secretary and editor, a combined role that proved difficult to manage. Production and mailing issues plagued the first year of the magazine under Bostrom.

The new relationship was bumpy at the beginning. Stanfield later wrote: "I became a Torch director just as the era of part-time executive secretaries and editors with veteran Torch backgrounds was ending and a contract with an association management firm was beginning. It wasn't an easy transition for Torch or for the management firm."

In 1979-1980 the number of clubs slightly increased. In September 1979 the "Red Book" listed 105 clubs, of which three were in Canada. One new club was chartered in Winchester, Virginia, in March 1980. In May Carroll reported that the number of chartered clubs had increased from 101 to 103 while Torch membership had risen from 4,290 to 4,300. The IATC reported that educators constituted the largest professional category, followed by attorneys, clergymen, physicians, and engineers.

The 1980 Convention was held in Kalamazoo, Michigan, on May 21-24. Its theme was "The Troubled State of the Professions." Kalamazoo had suffered a tornado on May 13, but the convention did take place, attended by 128 members and sixty-four guests. Forty-eight clubs were represented.

The Paxton Lecture was given by John W. Allen on "Our Five Constitutions: Maybe It's Time for a Sixth." Allen, a lawyer, had presented his paper in October 1979 before the Kalamazoo Club. The first person named as an Honorary Lifetime Member was Lois Crayton who had served on *The Torch* editorial team from the late 1940s to early 1960s. The President's Award was presented to the Lincoln Torch Club. The Nashville Club won the Most Improved Award.

Entertainment included walking tours of the Kalamazoo Mall, Bronson Park's cultural center, the Upjohn Company, antique shops, and the Paw Paw Wineries. Western Michigan University's string quartet gave a concert.

July 1980-June 1981

Leadership included President Fred R. Whaley, Jr. (administrator), President Elect Everett H. Hopkins (administrator/educator), Vice President Clarence A. Peterson (investment portfolio manager), Immediate Past President Clifton E. Rodgers (landscape architect), and Directors Alice M. Rohr, John M. Adams, Thatcher S. Wood, Leonard Josephson, Paul Stanfield, and Robert S. Rosow. Editor Lee Hoffman was replaced by David G. Lister, from Bostrom, who also served as executive secretary.

In June *The Torchlight* reported that the May 1980 Convention had approved a regional development program. Each regional director was to appoint a sufficient number of regional coordinators to provide IATC communications and support to each club. President Rodgers said the volunteer-staffed plan would strengthen bonds between the clubs and the IATC and would foster the growth of Torch. An external factor, however, was the 13.5 percent national inflation rate in 1980, which challenged the association, the clubs, and their members.

A year and a half into the new relationship with Bostrom, IATC President Elect Everett Hopkins declared, "I am convinced, even more than I was two years ago, that it was a mistake to put our affairs in the hands of a commercial outfit with no special interests in, or dedication to, the purposes of TORCH." *The Torch* editor Paxton frankly expressed similar misgivings.

In *The Torch* Hopkins observed that Torch membership continued to decline, and a high priority must go to reversing that trend. In the winter issue of *The Torchlight*, however, he noted an increase. He proposed to televise a Torch panel.

WINTER 1980

SPRING/SUMMER 1988

Fall 1999

Spring 2009

Winter 2020

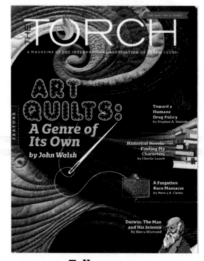

Fall 2023

The changing faces of *The Torch*

The board, meeting in March 1981, expressed concern at the delayed publication of *The Torch* and *The Torchlight*. It created a twelve-member Torch Magazine Editorial Advisory Board. Its financial report had an operating deficit of $8,863.

In its June 1981 meeting, the board called for more structure, guidelines, and deadlines on all its members to reverse IATC membership decline. It revoked the Tampa Club's charter for non-payment of dues. It put off forming a Torch Advisory Council until funding became available. The board raised dues to $20.

The October 1980 "Red Book" listed 102 clubs, with three in Canada. At the same time, the executive committee reported a membership of 4,237, a loss of 116 since the 1979 Convention report. In *The Torchlight* for June 1981 Carroll wrote that 57 percent of Torch Club charters resulted from the efforts of paid organizers (but, of these, one-third lasted for less than ten years), whereas volunteers brought in 35 percent, and extension efforts by existing clubs led to 8 percent. It was reported that Torch had added 282 members but lost 491; added three clubs including Cleveland and Omaha, but lost the Rockingham, Virginia, Club.

The 1981 Convention was held in Washington, DC, June 3-6. Its theme was "Our Government: Checks and Balances." It was attended by 139 members from thirty-six clubs.

The Paxton Lecture by John F. Brown Jr. was "Environmental Theology." It had been delivered to the Schenectady Torch Club in January 1981. The Outstanding Club Award went to Columbus.

In its meeting on June 5, the board, noting the low attendance at the Washington, DC Convention, appointed a twelve-member Torch Advisory Council. Meanwhile, a proposed International Advisory Council for the IATC was announced but not implemented due to lack of funds.

This convention included a VIP tour of the White House and a tour of the Capitol. Groups visited the Smithsonian Natural History Museum, the National Shrine of the Immaculate Conception, and the Japanese and Indonesian Embassies. The Swiss Folklore Group entertained the attenders with dancing and singing.

July 1981-June 1982

Leadership included President Everett H. Hopkins (educator), Immediate Past President Fred R. Whaley, Jr. (administrator), Vice President and Director at Large Paul Stanfield (editorial writer), President Elect Clarence A. Peterson (investment manager), Editor and Executive Secretary David Lister (replaced by Raymond C. Appel in February 1981), Archivist Thomas L. Carroll, Directors Alice M. Rohr (psychologist), John M. Adams (insurance underwriter), Thatcher S. Wood (chartered underwriter), Leonard M. Josephson (agronomist), David W. Crowner (dentist), and D. Orval Strong (minister).

In October 1981 *The Torchlight* reported that the board had approved two awards for next year: Outstanding Torch Member, and the Torch Award to the individual who had given exceptional service to Torch in the previous year.

The IATC still worried about the declining number of clubs and membership, although there had been a brief uptick earlier in 1981. The board and Bostrom were interested in forming an advisory board of internationally known figures but put off the project due to insufficient funds. It did try to form one in March 1982.

In a February 1982 meeting with Bostrom Management Corporation, IATC President Hopkins complained of a lack of communication between Executive Secretary David Lister and Torch members. President Elect Peterson said he had received no information about current dues collection and delinquent clubs. There had been no action taken on membership development. Reported membership figures were inadequate. *The Torch* magazine had blank pages and too many photos, with overly long biographies. Lister was replaced in February by Raymond C. Appel. This reduced strain between Bostrom and the Torch central office. The IATC, after Carroll's retirement, had wanted to centralize and modernize office functions and make use of computer databases and word processing available with a management firm. In *My Life in Torch*, Carroll admitted that the association should have tried to better communicate its needs to Bostrom.

The Torchlight's Spring 1982 issue noted that IATC had convened a special panel to examine its financial condition, which had been exacerbated by inflation and membership decline. President Hopkins hoped to bring recommendations for change to the Knoxville Convention.

The board discussed creation of an advisory board for *The Torch*, but deferred action until funding was available. In March 1982 however, the board named twelve members to *The Torch* Advisory Board.

The winter issue of *The Torch* noted that 1981 was the first time in many years that there was an increase in the number of clubs and members. However, at the end of the year the IATC reported 103 clubs, and membership had declined from 4,301 to 4,094. The York, Pennsylvania, Club elected to leave the IATC.

The 1982 Convention met in Knoxville, Tennessee, on June 15-18. Its theme was "Energy Turns the World." This meeting coincided with the Knoxville World's Fair, featuring wind and solar energy. One hundred and sixty members attended.

The Lecture was presented by Robert E. Shepherd, Jr.; the title of his topic was "Should God reenter the Public School Classroom in America?" The Most Improved Club Award was presented to the Oakland County, Michigan, Club. Frank J. O'Connor of the Norfolk Club was the first winner of the Outstanding Member and Torch Awards.

The 1982 Convention was marked by considerable rancor and controversy among the delegates, especially regarding the IATC's perceived decline. The year 1981-1982 seems to have been a nadir in the IATC's history. Several years of deficit spending had eroded the association's net worth. The board, responding to this challenge, decided that it must revise the constitution and bylaws yet again. It formed a committee to recommend procedures for changing them.

At its meeting during the convention, the board issued several directives: *The Torch* was to contain no more than eleven articles and thirty-six pages; *The Torch* and *The Torchlight* should each produce three issues annually. The board proposed to raise dues to $20 and have each club pay a $25 convention fee. It asked the Torch Foundation to underwrite *The Torch*. The board, concerned about the continuing decline of IATC membership, called for more structure, guidelines, and deadlines so that all officers and directors would know what was required and by when.

Excursions included a tour of Oak Ridge and a luncheon address by F.S. Patton, its Director of Engineering.

July 1982-June 1983

Leadership included President Clarence A. Peterson (investment manager), President Elect Paul Stanfield (editorial writer), Immediate Past President Everett H. Hopkins (educator), Directors Alice M. Rohr (psychologist), Chauncey Depuy (lawyer), Robert L. Stern (professor), Leonard M. Josephson (agronomist/educator), David W. Crowner (dentist), and Robert S. Rosow (CPA), Archivist Charles Atcher, Executive Secretary Raymond C. Appel (from Bostrom), Editor Art Grasior, and Cynthia Cipov (from Bostrom).

In the October-November 1982 issue of *The Torchlight* President Peterson stated that the IATC's financial situation had become dire. Its transition to Bostrom Management had proven very costly. IATC had run a deficit for several years while membership declined, which aggravated the fiscal problem. The president also noted that convention attendance had fallen. Typically, fewer than half the clubs were represented and only 2 percent of the membership. Peterson referred to the uproar at the Knoxville Convention, where delegates tried to amend the constitution without giving prior notice and expressed consternation about the IATC's financial situation.

The board appointed Depuy to chair a committee to study how the IATC should make changes in its constitution and bylaws. In April 1983 the board rejected a proposal to amend the constitution to give management of the IATC to the annual convention, which would impair the association's work between conventions. The board approved changing the IATC bylaws to extend the president and president elect's terms from one to two years, shorten those of directors from three years to two, and to abolish the office of vice president.

At the June 1983 board meeting, Crowner proposed to take over the position of executive secretary from Bostrom, answered questions about the budget and his facilities, and then left the meeting. The remaining board members discussed his proposal but voted to keep their existing arrangement with the Bostrom Corporation.

The board discussed contacts with the diplomatic community in Washington, DC. They also discussed forming clubs outside the US, possibly starting in Monterey, Mexico, or on military bases. The board also resolved to appoint a member to serve as liaison to the Torch Foundation. Past President Hopkins agreed to work with each regional director who needed help with "saving troubled clubs." The board resolved to give bonus points toward the President's Award to any club that played a leading part in forming a new club.

The "Red Book" in October 1982 listed ninety-seven clubs, with three in Canada. The October-November 1982 issue of *The Torchlight* reported that membership had declined from 4,094 to 3,975. In April the board reported that the Quad Cities, Virginia, Club had dissolved. Also the Ithaca, New York, Club had dropped out.

The 1983 Convention met in Albany and Schenectady, New York, July 13-15. Its theme was "Genetic Engineering." Forty-one clubs were represented by fifty-nine delegates and four alternates. The total convention attendance was 134.

The Paxton Lecture by Harry D. Lewis was "Is Your T.V. Watching You?" Lewis, an attorney, had originally presented this paper to the Nashville Club in October 1982. The President's Award was presented to the Columbus, Ohio, Club. The most Improved Club Award was presented to the Chattanooga, Tennessee, Club. The Outstanding Torch Member Award was given to Norman M. Howden of the Rochester, New York, Club, and the Outstanding Member Award for 1982 was presented retroactively to Tom Carroll, who had been unable to attend the Knoxville Convention.

The business meeting approved the proposed changes to the constitution and bylaws and increased dues to $25. The start of IATC's fiscal year was changed from December to June. *The Torch* was to be redesigned, starting with the January 1984 issue, and *The Torchlight* was reduced to two issues per year.

Entertainment consisted of a dinner cruise on Lake George, tours of the New York State Capitol, and a ballet.

Following the convention, a board member remarked that the event should have been better supervised by the board and the executive secretary but cited no cause for his complaint. The Board did award a certificate to Albany's Wayne Davis and his convention committee, but also formed a committee to compile new convention guidelines by September 30 for the 1984 Convention planners.

July 1983-June 1984

Leadership included President Clarence A. Peterson (investment portfolio administrator), President Elect Paul Stanfield (editorial writer), Immediate Past President Everett H. Hopkins (professor), Directors Richard R. Lynch (government), Chauncey M. Depuy (lawyer), Robert L. Stern (professor), Morrison Loewenstein (professor), David W. Crowner (dentist), Robert S.

Rosow (CPA), Director at Large Dr. Paul P. Cooke, Executive Secretary Raymond C. Appel (Bostrom), Editor Eve Bradley (Bostrom), and Archivist Charles Atcher.

President Peterson expressed concern about low attendance at IATC conventions and called for regional mini-meetings.

In its September-October 1983 issue *The Torchlight* and the "Red Book" published the revised constitution and bylaws that had been approved unanimously at the 1983 Convention. The main changes approved were clauses in Article VI stating that the IATC's <u>governance</u> was vested in the member clubs through the official delegates at duly-called conventions, while its <u>management</u> was the responsibility of the officers and the board. The list of eligible professions was retained.

The "Red Book" of October 1983 reported ninety-four clubs, with three in Canada. There were at this time around 3,900 Torch members.

The 1984 Convention met in Toledo, Ohio, June 27-30. Its theme was "Fresh Water—Our Most Precious Resource." One hundred delegates represented thirty-two clubs. Mayor Donna Owens of Toledo gave welcoming remarks.

The Paxton Lecture, delivered by Dan Pletta, was "Are Foxes Guarding the Hen House?" This paper was first presented to the Montgomery County, Virginia, Club on February 14, 1984. The Paxton Lectureship Competition Runner Up was awarded to Lou J. Briggs for "Sex and Politics." This paper was first presented to the Columbus Torch Club in March 1984. She had been the Associate Director of Children's Hospital Foundation and the Associate Director of Columbus Foundation.

Convention entertainment included lunch on a river boat on "the Mighty Maumee" or lunch at the Toledo Art Museum.

Chapter 2: July 1984–June 1994

Written by Paul Scott Stanfield
Researched by Raimund Goerler

Decade Overview

The looming question for Torch in its seventh decade was essentially that of the preceding and following decades—a continuing gradual decline in the number of clubs and in the overall membership. Total membership stood at 3,561 in September 1984, a serious decline from the 5,000-plus figure of the late 1960s, and declined further to 3,002 by 1994. The total number of clubs declined from eighty-nine to seventy-nine. At least one new club was chartered (Rockford, Illinois, in 1991), and a club that had left IATC reaffiliated (Auburn, New York, in 1988), but more clubs disbanded. In 1991-1992 alone Torch lost the Chattanooga, Tallahassee, Wabash Valley, and Indianapolis Clubs.

The basic mechanism of the decline was easy to identify. The many who had joined Torch in the rapid growth years of 1955-1965 were now quite a bit older and going the way of all flesh, but younger members were not joining in numbers sufficient to make up the losses. The plaintive note sounded in the last official communication of the Laguna Hills, California, Torch Club, dated March 22, 1984, could have found an echo in a good many other Torch Clubs that disbanded during this period:

> Our Torch Club has been in financial difficulties and plagued with loss of membership over the past three years, primarily due to our members dying. The average age was over seventy-five years old.

> Last fall they raised the price of our meals to $9 with a $325 minimum per meeting. This meant we needed at least thirty-six present at each meeting and then we were a dollar short. The members did not want to change our meeting place though the club often had to pay to make the minimum.

> At our last meeting, March 19, we announced we were broke, would have a $15 a year increase in dues ... and we needed a new secretary. (I took the job in 1980 when I was president and the secretary suddenly died. I couldn't find someone to take the job so I resigned as President and took the job myself.) Four years is enough.

One Region 1 club, which was down to fifteen members, met at the retirement facility where most of the members lived—convenient for them, certainly, but an awkward place to which to invite prospective new members. Another Region 1 club was down to five members. They met only five times a year, with each member giving a paper every year—admirable persistence, but, unsurprisingly, the club did not last. The Fall 1986 issue of *The Torch* contained an article on the same theme: "The Demise of the Essex County Torch Club (NJ)," by C. DeWitt

Boney, which warned against "cloistering" and recommended that "Torch needs a provocative purpose...."

Concerted efforts to understand and address the problem of eroding membership bookended this period. In 1979-1981, Region 3 Director Thatcher Wood led a Special Membership Project that involved outreach to every club via the regional directors (with suggested phone scripts) as well as a list of general strategies, e.g.: "7. Admit women. The walls are crumbling. A valuable resource, overlooked by many clubs." More women did join Torch, but the overall downward trend held, leading to the "Vision 2000" project of 1996-1997 and its report, which acknowledged, "It is possible that clubs just didn't keep their eye on the ball."

The problem of declining membership was hardly unique to Torch, however. Other fraternal and service organizations were noticing the same trends and asking themselves the same questions. In *Democracy in America* Alexis de Tocqueville had identified voluntary civil associations as a distinctive ingredient in the success of the American democratic experiment: "But what political power could ever hope to equal the countless multitude of small ventures in which American citizens participate every day through their associations?" In the last quarter of the twentieth century that looked to be changing. It may have been not just that eyes were not kept on the ball, but that the whole game—the whole culture—had changed.

Although the number of members was getting smaller during this period, it seems fair to say that the Torch experience suffered no diminution at all. In the years 1984 to 1994, Torch enjoyed a series of strong, generally well-attended conventions, continued to produce a vital, interesting magazine, and had the benefits of stable, conscientious leadership. Torch was not growing, true, but in other respects it was healthy.

The most remarkable membership development in this period bore on the long-evolving story of the inclusion of women in Torch. By 1974 most clubs had exercised what was called the "local option" and admitted women members, and by 1981 two women, Anthea Duron and Alice Rohr, had served on the board. In 1991 the big question was whether a club could exercise a "local option" to remain all-male. By one count, there were six clubs that did not admit women. The San Antonio Club and the Athens, Georgia, Club were among the six, and strong contingents in both clubs wanted to keep it that way, even if that meant withdrawing from the IATC. At the 1991 Convention in Buffalo, Leo G. Macpherson of the Baltimore Club moved the following amendment to Article III of the IATC Constitution: "Section 3. Gender shall not be a criterion for acceptance or denial of membership in the Association or in any Torch club." Chauncey Depuy, who had proposed admitting women thirty-nine years before, seconded. The question was "passionately debated" at the 1991 Convention in Buffalo, according to eyewitness Reed Taylor. Some saw gender discrimination as a "moral issue" that had to be resolved; others saw the amendment as an imposition on club autonomy: "Under its present organizational structure, the association cannot compel a club to accept or reject anyone for membership," wrote Art Palmer in a letter to the editor of *The Torch*. The diplomacy of President George Crepeau and his successor Richard Lynch were crucial, Taylor thought, to the compromise in which the all-male clubs would adjust their bylaws to allow the eligibility of women to apply for membership but could for the time being defer any active soliciting of such applications. Dick Lynch is modest about his own role in this, saying that the formerly all-male clubs "ultimately came around" mainly because they saw that remaining male-only "wasn't worth the struggle" and they "just got tired." At the 1992 Convention in Columbus a proposal to revise the bylaws into gender-neutral language passed handily. The change in the bylaws seems to have adequately addressed the question of the eligibility of women, as the idea of amending the IATC Constitution was dropped.

Generally, presidential succession in the 1984-94 period worked just as designed. An engaged and capable regional director was invited to stand as a candidate for president elect; once elected, that person would serve two years on the board as president elect, then two years as president, then two as immediate past president. The potential for strong continuity in such an arrangement is obvious, and so it proved in the easy and cordial transitions from Paul S. Stanfield of the Des Moines Club and a former Region 7 Director and Publications Chair, to Robert S. Rosow of the San Antonio Club and a former director at large, to John M. Adams of the Lehigh Valley Club and a former Region 2 Director, to George P. Crepeau of the Columbus, Ohio, Club and a former Region 5 Director, to Richard R. Lynch of the Albany Club and a former Region 1 Director. The sole hitch occurred when Dean C. Gross of the South Hampton Roads Club and a former Region 3 Director, president elect in 1992-94, suffered major health reverses and was unable to take office as president in 1994. Former Region 1 Director F. Reed Taylor of the Buffalo Club then stepped up and served as acting president in 1994-95 and duly served his own two-year term in 1995-1997.

One former president attributed the harmonious and collegial transfers of power of this period to "a strong sense of friendship and a common cause. We were all in it for the good of Torch, all devoted to that cause." The spirit of co-operation and shared mission that prevailed meant that the Torch experience remained healthy and vital even as numbers declined.

In the mid-1980s Bostrom management continued to handle routine activities of the IATC. Some Bostrom employees assigned to Torch grasped its spirit and *ethos* sufficiently to pursue their work with real dedication. One such person was Carol Estey, who served as executive secretary from 1985 to 1990. Paul Stanfield later wrote of the gratitude he felt "that someone up in the Tribune Tower was giving Torch matters a special kind of attention." The board voted to offer Estey special recognition, and at the September 29, 1990 meeting she was awarded a plaque bearing an original limerick:

> Hail to the person from Tribune Tower
> Who brought to the Torch Clubs great light and power
> So cheerful and zesty
> We'll miss Carol Estey
> Her tireless efforts made all of Torch flower!

Among the functions assumed by Bostrom in the early 1980s was editing *The Torch*. The first few years were rocky, the new editors being neither professional journalists nor familiar with the traditions of Torch, but the ship was righted with the arrival of Eve Bradley as editor in 1984. "Eve is the first trained and experienced journalist to handle the magazine for Bostrom," wrote Publications Chair and President Elect Stanfield to a correspondent in 1984. "I was disappointed that I was not consulted the way I should have been at the time of the change, but she has had quite a mess to clean up—and at least has our publications on schedule for the first time since the management change."

The restoration of order begun by Bradley was successfully sustained by Jeanne Marks McDonald, who became editor with the Fall 1984/Winter 1985 issue. She too was a Bostrom employee, but she seemed to have caught the spirit of Torch. She attended not only the conventions, as all the Bostrom-employed editors did, but also some meetings of the Chicago Club, which her husband eventually joined. McDonald was a main mover in the decision to use images on the cover of the magazine, a practice maintained during her 1985-91 tenure (then dropped until 2013). She also instituted the "Editor's Quill Award," a kind of companion to the Paxton, given to the paper the editor deemed best among those published in that year's volume of the magazine. There were six winners—E. N. Brandt (1985), David O. Rankin (1986), Richard L. Rice (1987), Chauncey M. Depuy (1988), Mahlon H. Hellerich (1989), and Willis P. Whichard (1990)—but the award seems to have ended with McDonald's editorship. In the "P.S." column of the Spring 1991 issue, the last she edited, Stanfield wrote of her taking "a special interest in Torch and understanding the spirit behind it." He continued: "This, with a high-level competence in the editorial field, soon made the magazine something we have all shown with pride. At least I have, even though I had to be embarrassed by the credit sometime given to me as publications chair. It was Jeanne who made the difference."

In that same issue, McDonald wrote in her final "From the Editor's Desk" column: "As editor of *The Torch* magazine for almost six years, I can say it has been one of the most rewarding experiences of my career. I have enjoyed tremendously and learned so much reading the many outstanding papers that have been submitted to *The Torch*."

McDonald was succeeded by Susan Moss, who helmed the magazine capably from 1991 through the end of 1993 and brought to it something of McDonald's enthusiasm. Philip Lesser served as editor of one issue, Winter 1994, while also serving as executive secretary. The magazine typically received between forty and fifty submissions a year during this period. Forty years later, that would sound like an abundant haul, but it seemed thin at the time: "We are in desperate need of papers to be submitted for the Torch magazine," pleaded the Executive Secretary Raymond Appel in *The Torchlight* of February 1985. At the beginning of the 1984-1985 period, the board decided to cut back the number of issues per year from four to three.

The content of *The Torch* during 1984-1994 continued to present a rich array of well-informed and insightful articles on a remarkable range of topics: poetry to physics, political theory to medical ethics, genetics, economics, and more. While the articles were often by scholars and always informed by scholarship, they were not written by specialists for other specialists, but addressed to an educated, thoughtful, intellectually curious reader—*The Torch* reader, in short. There were even a few personal essays, like Tom Carroll's 1992 "Anatomy of a Profession," which reflected on the dubious reputation of his public relations profession, or Lynn Dickerson's 1993 "Confessions of an Appalachian Tree Farmer." Torch being Torch, a paper might be based on personal experience yet also make a bold argument. "Homosexuality: A View from the Pulpit" from 1992 is a case in point. A Methodist minister and member of the Des Moines Club, Larry W. Sonner, described his lengthy, scholarly, and soul-searching progress towards the conclusion that "[t]here is not sufficient biblical evidence to convince me that homosexuality in and of itself is sin." In a 1991 column Stanfield wrote that "as a rule, a Torch paper should present a thesis, an opinion about the subject, a point of view which is supported and illuminated by the content the speaker has brought together from his or her life experience and research." The papers of this era did not avoid controversy, since as Stanfield pointed out, the primary goal of a Torch paper was "the stimulation of a lively discussion."

In 1990 controversy swirled around an article by Charles E. Marthinsen of the Harrisburg, Pennsylvania, Club titled "The Middle East Dilemma." Marthinsen, who had retired from the Foreign Service, was certainly direct: "In my experience, the United States government, both the Executive and Legislative branches, and the American electorate have indulged towards Israel an habitual fondness that has made us slaves." Strongly worded responses followed from Henry Heimansohn of the Indianapolis Club and Jack Bloom of the Western South Carolina Club, followed by a response-to-the-responses from Marthinsen himself. But Marthinsen's was not the only article to stir editorial correspondence. The Winter 1987/88 issue contained a challenging response to Cabell Brand's "America, the Strong"—a Paxton winner, no less. Perhaps the most forceful challenge to a Paxton-winning paper occurred at the 1993 Convention in Portland, Maine, when an audience member arose immediately after the delivery of Charles Beaudette's "Cold Fusion and the Press" to declare that the author was "perpetuating a scientific fraud."

All the magazine's editors in the 1984-94 period worked with the Editorial Advisory Committee that had been created in 1980-81 under the direction of Publications Chair Stanfield. Since these editors were employees of Bostrom, they had limited or no familiarity with the culture of Torch. Creating the advisory board likely did a great deal to preserve the magazine's ability to represent that culture.

By 1992-1993 the relationship between Bostrom and Torch was fraying. There were concerns about transparency in billing and accounting matters, and more generally suspicion that IATC was not receiving the kind of attention it deserved from its management firm. The tone of some of the correspondence suggests that Bostrom was not happy either. In October 1992 Robert Tonia, Executive Secretary at Bostrom, wrote to President Lynch: "I wish to point out that if a client with the same budget were to hire Bostrom today, the fixed fees would total $10,350 more than IATC is paying for the same services." By 1993 Torch leadership was seeking a new management firm.

Dean Gross, the 1992-1994 president elect whose health issues prevented him from assuming the office of president, turned out to have the answer. A member of the South Hampton Roads Club, Gross was familiar with the work of Strickland and Jones, P.C., a small but capable firm that he thought would do well for IATC. At an executive session on June 24 of the 1994 Norfolk Convention it was resolved that Torch would terminate its relationship with Bostrom and engage Strickland and Jones as its management firm.

Gale and Jimmy Strickland

James V. (Jimmy) Strickland was officially executive secretary, but his wife Gale, officially the administrative assistant, was "the person on the ground who did all the work." Her lilting Southern accent soon became familiar to Torch directors and officers across the country. The smaller scale of Strickland and Jones allowed for the development of a more personal, involved relationship with IATC than had been possible with Bostrom. "Jimmy and Gail were a wonderful team," recalled one past president. "They had a real sense of the organization, and Torch was not just an account for them." The relationship, which the same past president described as "wonderful," lasted until 2010, when the Stricklands retired. Patrick Deans, a longtime member of the Norfolk Club who sometimes did legal consulting for Strickland and Jones, became editor of *The Torch*.

JULY 1984-JUNE 1985

Leadership included President Paul S. Stanfield, Past President Clarence Peterson, and President Elect Robert S. Rosow (also Region 6 Director). The remainder of the board included Richard Lynch (Region 1), Chauncey Depuy (Region 2), Robert L. Stern (Region 3), Morris Lowenstein (Region 4), John W. Allen (Region 5), and Paul P. Cooke (Director-at-Large). Carol Estey served as executive secretary, and Jeanne McDonald was editor of *The Torch*.

In June of 1985 membership stood at 3,577 (3,481 regular members, ninety-five emeritus, and two honorary). Two clubs disbanded and none were chartered, for a total of eighty-nine clubs.

The 1985 Convention was held in Des Moines, Iowa, June 19-21. The decision to hold the convention west of the Mississippi was considered risky, given the geographical distribution of Torch clubs. At the St. Paul Convention of 1974, marking Torch's 50th anniversary in the city of the very first club, attendance was disappointing. But attendance at the 1985 Convention was healthy at 166 attendees, and the meeting was marked by "fellowship and neighborly good spirits."

The Paxton Lecture was "Dance Band on the Titanic" by Jerry L. Petr of the Lincoln, Nebraska, Club, on income inequality.

It was announced that the board had voted unanimously to award a Lifetime Honorary Membership to Norris Paxton. No bylaws changes occurred at this convention.

Trips and activities included visits to Living History Farms, the Botanical Center ("a tropical wonderland under a 150-foot dome") and the production *Of Mice and Men* by the Des Moines Metro Opera.

JULY 1985-JUNE 1986

Leadership included President Paul S. Stanfield, Past President Clarence Peterson, and President Elect Robert S. Rosow. The remainder of the board included Richard Lynch, Harold W. Thompson, Jr., Robert L. Stern, Morris Lowenstein, John W. Allen, Richard Rosen, and Charles Beorn. Carol Estey served as executive secretary, and Jeanne McDonald was editor of *The Torch*.

The minutes of the June 29, 1986, board meeting recorded a concern that the actions of the Torch Foundation had "not been in line with its original intent" and that the board should "recapture the Foundation." The possibility of creating a second endowment for IATC was discussed. (Chapter 6 of this history contains a more detailed discussion of the Foundation.)

In June 1986 membership stood at 3,562 (3,481 regular members, 101 Emeritus, six At-Large, and three Honorary). Two clubs disbanded (Essex, New Jersey, and Windsor, Ontario) but one club (Auburn, New York) re-affiliated, for a total of eighty-eight clubs.

The 1986 Convention was held in Richmond, Virginia, June 29-July 2. The relatively large size of the club meant it could provide many volunteers and the convention was well-organized. Rosow observed, "Torch conventions are always great, but the Richmond Renaissance this year was exceptional." There was an uptick in attendance to 185.

The Paxton winner was "Genes, Again" by John H. T. Bryan of the Athens, Georgia Club on genetic engineering. Other papers included "Beyond Ronald Reagan," and "Ethics in Industry."

No bylaws were changed at this convention.

The tours took full advantage of the region's deep history, taking in Monumental Avenue, Tuckahoe Plantation (Thomas Jefferson's boyhood home), the Virginia State Capitol, Wilton House (home of the Randolphs), Maymont Mansion, and Hollywood Cemetery. Seven professional actors re-created the scene of Patrick Henry's famous "Give Me Liberty, or Give Me Death" speech at the Colonial Convention.

JULY 1986-JUNE 1987

Leadership included President Robert S. Rosow, Past President Paul Stanfield, and President Elect John M. Adams. The remainder of the board included Richard Lynch (Region 1), Harold W. Thompson, Jr. (Region 2), Robert L. Stern (Region 3), John R. Barry (Region 4), George P. Crepeau (Region 5), Corwin D. Moore (Region 6), and Richard Rosen (Director-at-Large). Carol Estey remained as executive secretary, and Jeanne McDonald as editor of *The Torch*.

In a special meeting of the board of directors held on July 1, 1986, Rosow explained to new board members that the previous board had decided to request the resignations of all current trustees of the Torch Foundation and install new trustees. (For details see Chapter 6.) The board approved a motion to obtain in writing the language of an agreement made among President Rosow, Clarence Peterson, and Forrest Smith of the Foundation.

In April 1987 membership stood at 3,478. The Pike's Peak Club returned their charter.

The 1987 Convention was held in Akron, Ohio, June 24-26. The hotel chosen was particularly memorable—the Quaker Square Hilton Inn was a converted grain elevator. One attendee recalled the Akron Convention as "one of my favorites," another fondly remembered that one Torch member who worked in security operations found a way to sneak food and drink into the hotel's pool area.

The Paxton Lecture was "America, the Strong," by E. Cabell Brand of the Roanoke Valley, Virginia, Club on adopting the elimination of poverty as a national policy goal. Other papers included "The One-Newspaper Town," "City at the Summit," "Does the Rust Belt Have a Future?," "Polymers in Your Future," and "Takeover Ordeal."

Past IATC President Taylor noted that "a good thing about Torch conventions is that they are not strictly according to the Visitors' Bureau. You get an insider's tour of the city." The convention's sights included not only the famous Goodyear Blimp, but also the Akron Civic Theater, the Kent State University Fashion Museum, the Football Hall of Fame, and the Stan Hywet Manor House.

JULY 1987-JUNE 1988

Leadership included President Robert S, Rosow, Past President Paul Stanfield, and President Elect John M. Adams. The remainder of the board included Richard Lynch (Region 1), Harold

W. Thompson, Jr. (Region 2), Charles Beorn (Region 3), John R. Barry (Region 4), George P. Crepeau (Region 5), Corwin D. Moore (Region 6), and Richard Rosen (Director-at-Large). Carol Estey remained as executive secretary, and Jeanne McDonald as editor of *The Torch*.

In May of 1988 membership stood at 3,420.

The 1988 Convention was held in the Bay City-Saginaw, Michigan, area, June 15-18. A tornado had been through the week before the convention, and there was some concern as to whether the facilities would be available and ready, but in the end it was "one of the best conventions ever." Registered attendance came to 161.

The Paxton Lecture was "The Delicate Threads of Life" by Hubert J. Davis of the Portsmouth, Virginia, Club on human-caused degradation of the natural environment. Other paper topics included local history and the medical and surgical uses of silicon.

Executive Secretary Carol Estey proposed that "a professional study and analysis could be performed" to see what it would take to increase membership and add clubs. Better communication of Torch's existence and strengths, she thought, would make a difference.

Tours included the Michigan Division of Dow Chemical, the Dow Gardens, a "Factory of the Future," and the Japanese Tea House.

JULY 1988-JUNE 1989

Leadership included President John M. Adams, Past President Robert Rosow, and President Elect George Crepeau. Directors were Richard Lynch (Region 1), Harold W. Thompson, Jr. (Region 2), Charles Beorn (Region 3), Warren F. Spencer (Region 4), Jack M. Ryder (Region 5), Corwin D. Moore (Region 6), and Richard Rosen (Director-at-Large). Carol Estey remained as executive secretary, and Jeanne McDonald as editor of *The Torch*.

A special meeting of the board was held on September 25 to discuss a proposal from Bostrom Management that addressed the topics raised by the executive secretary's report at the 1988 Convention and suggested the additional services that Bostrom could provide. The consensus of the board was that the proposal was "unacceptable." The board continued to pursue the topic of new efforts at development over the next year, including the drafting of new brochures.

In May of 1989 membership stood at 3,320, in eighty-three clubs.

Attendance at the 1989 Convention, June 28-July 1, the first for Torch in San Antonio, did not suffer from the travel distance required, with 170 attendees and guests. Those who attended remembered it vividly. The convention hotel was right across the street from the Alamo. One attendee recalled the convention as "very, very nice," another as "lavish." It somewhat exceeded its budget. (They do things big in Texas.)

The Paxton-winning paper was "The Paradymes of Change," on the subject of change and response to change, by Warner M. Montgomery of the St. Catharines, Ontario, Club.

Montgomery may have devoted much of his time to another subject, however. As "A Critique on the 1989 Convention" by Thomas Carroll emphatically states, "Never again should any Paxton Award winner be permitted to depart from the paper for which the award was given." (The departure perhaps occasioned the very resistance to change that the original paper had discussed.)

At the first business session the delegates approved raising by $10 the dues paid by each member of Torch to IATC. The board also approved providing a $250 subsidy as incentive for each club to send at least one delegate, hoping not only to achieve wider representation at the convention but also to make sure more Torch members experienced a convention for themselves and thus better understood the benefits of IATC affiliation.

At the 1989 Convention two changes to the bylaws were proposed. The first—deletion of the clause in Bylaw I, Section C, that read "and who are known to be intellectually alert, socially companionable and financially responsible"—fell short of approval. The second—changing the position of Bylaw VIII, Section 3 (regarding emeritus membership) so that it became Bylaw I, Section 5—passed unanimously.

Attendees enjoyed walking tours of the Alamo, the River Walk, and Germantown.

The tradition of passing an elaborately-phrased resolution thanking the convention's hosts and organizers at the final business session may have begun in San Antonio. The text of the resolution, written by Paul Stanfield, later appeared in the Fall 1989 *Torchlight*.

JULY 1989-JUNE 1990

Leadership included President John M. Adams, Past President Robert Rosow, and President Elect George Crepeau. The remainder of the board included Richard Lynch (Region 1), Harold W. Thompson, Jr. (Region 2), Hubert J. Davis (Region 3), Warren F. Spencer (Region 4), Jack M. Ryder (Region 5), Corwin D. Moore (Region 6), and Richard Rosen (Director-at-Large). Carol Estey remained as executive secretary, and Jeanne McDonald as editor of *The Torch*.

The dues increase approved at the 1989 Convention unsurprisingly caused dissatisfaction among some clubs, which the board discussed over the fall and winter meetings. The unhappiness seemed to die down as the year progressed.

In June of 1990, President Adams reported to the board on the progress Carroll was making in his history of the first fifty years of Torch, and the board discussed ways of publishing and distributing this work.

The 1990 Convention was held in Bethlehem, Pennsylvania, June 27-30. It was on the smaller side as far as convention sites go, but the Lehigh Valley Club put on "a wonderful convention" according to one of the 150 attendees.

The Paxton Lecture was "Professionalism on the Rocks," by Jesse R. Long, of the Toledo, Ohio, Club on the public's loss of confidence in the authority of "professionals" and other elites. Taking as its theme "Building Community in the 21st Century," the program included the papers "The History of Moravian Bethlehem," "The Future of the American Steel Industry," "The Future of Atomic Energy in the American Economy," "The University and Economic Development," "The Pennsylvania Germans and Their Culture," and "The Ethical Foundations of Community."

Participants visited the Lehigh University Mountaintop Campus and took a walking tour of historic Bethlehem.

JULY 1990-JUNE 1991

Leadership included President George Crepeau, Past President John Adams, and President Elect Richard R. Lynch (also Region 1 Director). The remainder of the board included Harold W. Thompson, Jr. (Region 2), Hubert J. Davis (Region 3), Warren F. Spencer (Region 4), Robert S. P. Yien (Region 5), Corwin D. Moore (Region 6), and Richard Rosen (Director-at-Large). In February of 1991, Harold Thompson died. Chauncey Depuy took over as acting Region 2 Director. In the fall of 1990, Robert Tonai replaced Carol Estey as executive secretary. In the spring of 1991, Susan Moss replaced Jeanne McDonald as editor of *The Torch*. (These changes were made by Bostrom Management.)

Among President Crepeau's priorities in 1990-91 were revising the regional structure to improve communications and raising the membership's awareness of the Torch Foundation ("The Torch Foundation: Directions for the 1990s and Beyond" was published in 1991.)

In September 1990 membership stood at 3,424, an encouraging increase. However, membership fell again, standing at 3,014 in June 1991. The closure of several clubs, including Tallahassee, Chattanooga, and Indianapolis, probably accounted for much of the drop. A new club was chartered in the first half of 1991, in Rockford, Illinois.

The 1991 Convention in Buffalo, New York, June 26-29, showed an increase in attendance. There were 150 official attendees, not counting guests, who likely would have brought the total close to 200. Reed Taylor did such a masterful job as convention committee chair that he was asked to serve on the board of directors and eventually became IATC president.

The Paxton Lecture was "Iran: The Search for Utopia," by Ernest R. Olney, from the Winchester Club, on the Ayatollah Khomeini's attempt to create an ideal Islamic state. Congruent with the convention's theme, "Buffalo: A City of Frontiers," the papers presented included "Frontier in Environmental Management," "The Frontier of Free Trade," "The Passing of the North American Sport Frontier," and "Frontier of Research."

Several decisions were announced or ratified at the 1991 Convention, the most significant being a restructuring of the regions from six to twelve, the phasing out of the Emeritus dues category, the formation of a President's Advisory Council, and the decision to publish Carroll's history of Torch.

A moment vividly recalled later occurred during the Paxton banquet on the convention's final evening. President Crepeau was making some closing remarks on the theme of his presidency, "Rekindle the Flame of Torch," martini glass aloft, when a lit candle tipped over at the head table, starting a small fire. Crepeau nonchalantly tipped his martini onto the fire (a gesture more eloquent than efficacious, given the alcohol content of the average martini), which was soon extinguished thanks to some nearby water glasses, and then without missing a beat asked the attendees to keep this image in mind as they went home to rekindle the flame of Torch.

Tour destinations included the Botanical Gardens, the Albright Knox Art Gallery, the Welland Canal, a winery in neighboring St. Catharines, Ontario, Niagara-on-the-Lake, and quite a few more. Thursday's dinner was held on the S. S. Niagara Clipper.

JULY 1991-JUNE 1992

Leadership included President George Crepeau, Past President John Adams, and President Elect Richard R. Lynch. The remainder of the board included A. Reed Taylor (Region 1), Tej S. Saini (Region 2), Dean C. Gross (Region 3), Warren F. Spencer (Region 4), Robert S. P. Yien (Region 5), Corwin D. Moore (Region 6), and Richard Rosen (Director-at-Large). Robert Tonai continued as executive secretary, as did Susan Moss as editor of *The Torch.*

Membership had declined again by June 1992, to 2,890 (2,784 regular, ninety-two Emeritus, twelve At-Large, two Honorary). The Wabash Valley club closed, bringing the total number of clubs to eighty.

The 1992 Convention was held in Columbus, Ohio, on June 24-27. The quincentennial of Christopher Columbus's first voyage inspired both the choice of the convention site and its theme, "Celebrating Discovery." Columbus, home to one of Torch's larger and more vibrant clubs, was well situated to provide an excellent convention. Attendance, counting both members and guests, was over 200.

The Paxton Lecture was "Ownership of Human Tissue," by Kathryn P. Clausen, Columbus, on an issue of medical ethics with reference to the cell line later made famous in the bestseller *The Immortal Life of Henrietta Lacks.* Other papers included "Columbus Discovered," "The Entrepreneur, Technology, and Economic Development," "Turning on the Lights: Myths and Anti-Myths of the Quincentenary," "Treasures of a Lost Voyage," and "Simple Theories Seduce, Simplistic Theories Seduce Absolutely."

The convention approved a major revision of the bylaws, which were recast in gender-neutral language. The attendees also approved a constitutional amendment touching on the amendment process (Article VIII); in September the proposed amendment was forwarded to all the clubs for a final vote, in which it was approved by the general membership.

Tour destinations included German Village, the Brewer District, Thurber House, and of course The Ohio State University. A unique aspect of the convention was that for Wednesday night's dinner, convention attendees were invited to individual Columbus Club members' homes.

JULY 1992-JUNE 1993

Leadership included President Richard R. Lynch, Past President George Crepeau, and President Elect Dean C. Gross. The remainder of the board included A. Reed Taylor (Region 1), Tej S. Saini (Region 2), Bruce Souders (Region 3), Gayther L. Plummer (Region 4), Charles B. Hartley (Region 5), John V. Balian (Region 6), Ferd Anderson (of the newly created Region 7), and David Craig (Director-at-Large). Robert Tonai continued as executive secretary, as did Susan Moss as editor of *The Torch*.

The role and future of the Torch Foundation continued to be a concern of the board, as indicated by a June 1993 memo to the board from Peterson and Crepeau.

Membership rose very slightly by June of 1993, to 2,910 in seventy-nine clubs. A new club—Bucks County, in Pennsylvania—was reported in *Torchlight* as nearly ready to apply for its charter.

The 1993 Convention was held in Portland, Maine, June 23-26. For the third year in a row the total attendance of Torch members and guests exceeded 200. The official total of 223 was recognized as a new record for Torch conventions.

The gradual decline in national membership continued, however. As he had in Columbus in 1992, Lynch urged every club to make a goal of recruiting ten new members in the year ahead. (Columbus, Lehigh Valley, Albany, and Rochester actually met this goal, as reported at the next convention.)

The Paxton Lecture was "Cold Fusion and the Press," by Charles G. Beaudette, of the Western Maine Club. Other papers included "Success Begins with Education—And Education Begins with Us," "That Man on the White Horse," "Don't Take My Space!," "Doublespeak: Do We Really Mean What We Say?," and "Aging and Physical Capacity."

There were no new bylaws.

The "small but proud" club provided some classic regional experiences—a lobster dinner, a trip to a lighthouse, and shopping at L.L. Bean—suitable to the convention's theme, "Maine—The Way Life Should Be."

JULY 1993 -JUNE 1994

Leadership included President Richard R. Lynch, Past President George Crepeau, and President Elect Dean C. Gross. Health reasons prevented Gross from fulfilling his duties, and new President Elect A. Reed Taylor of the Buffalo Club served in his stead. The remainder of the board included A. Reed Taylor (Region 1), Tej S. Saini (Region 2), Bruce Souders (Region 3), Gayther L. Plummer (Region 4), Charles B. Hartley (Region 5), John V. Balian (Region 6), Ferd Anderson (Region 7), and David Craig (Director-at-Large). Robert Tonai continued as executive secretary, as did Susan Moss as editor of *The Torch*, until sometime between September and December in 1993, at which point Phillip Lesser became both executive secretary and editor. This change may have had to do with deteriorating relations with Bostrom.

A lingering question throughout the 1984-1994 period was finding a home for the Torch archives that had long been maintained in his own home by Carroll. On April 7, 1994, the board approved a proposal to house the archives in The Ohio State University Library, where they remain. Immediate Past President Crepeau was a key figure in this happy outcome.

The 1993-1994 year saw another increase in overall membership, to 3,002. The number of clubs remained at seventy-nine until Bucks County was presented with its charter at the 1994 Convention, bringing the number to eighty.

The 1994 Convention was held in Norfolk, Virginia, June 22-25. This convention marked the end of the Bostrom years for IATC and the beginning of the years of Strickland and Jones, which headquartered there. In the final business session, Lynch presented R. Patrick Deans, incoming editor of *The Torch*, to the convention.

The Paxton Lecture was "What Is the Function of Poetry?," by Thomas L. Minnick, of the Columbus, Ohio, Club. The author gave "a triumph over time" as one answer to its title's question.

No new bylaws were passed.

Norfolk's huge harbor and sprawling naval base made excellent tour destinations, as did Norfolk's having been the setting for events during the American Revolution and the Civil War.

Chapter 3: July 1994-June 2004

Written by Joseph Zawicki
Researched by Rich Davis

Decade Overview

The IATC faced several challenges during the decade running from 1994-2004. At the start of the decade there were approximately 3,000 Torch Club members in seventy-nine clubs. Membership issues in the mid-1990s were like those in earlier and later decades. Attempts were made to increase club membership numbers, but a lasting solution was yet to be found. By 2004 the membership had decreased to 2,485, a decline of around 17 percent from approximately 2,990 in 1994. New clubs were formed, but several closed over the decade. Maintaining membership continued to be an ongoing issue. By the end of the decade the issue of allowing women into Torch Clubs had been settled, and the idea of a "household" membership for a spouse or significant other was born. With a regular membership, a spouse could join for half price.

This decade saw the first woman elected as the IATC President—Ruth Giller, from Grand Rapids, Michigan. Additionally, several women were elected as presidents at the local level. Minority participation during this period was not well documented.

Leadership challenges came at the beginning of the new decade. Health issues caused an incoming president to resign before running his first meeting; in the true spirit of Torch, the president elect stepped up to the plate and admirably took over the reins of leadership.

The decade from July 1994 to June 2004 was remarkable on many levels. It also saw the first inklings of the electronic age. Initial steps were taken to develop websites, consider online meetings, and share recordings of presentations. We should applaud the efforts of the "early adopters" in our leadership. Communicating using online resources such as webpages and video recordings was a brave step forward.

A singular event that profoundly affected Torch and the nation also occurred in this decade: the 9/11 attacks. Wilbur Wright of the Buffalo, New York, Club reported on the impact of the terrorist attacks on the Twin Towers in New York City, the Pentagon in Washington, DC, and the crash of Flight 93 near Shanksville, Pennsylvania. The Buffalo Club had scheduled September 11 as their day to celebrate the 75th Anniversary of their founding. The Buffalo secretary, Art Hoekstra, was stranded at O'Hare Airport in Chicago. The St. Catharines, Ontario, contingent was planning to attend the celebration in Buffalo, but they were blocked at the international border. Buffalo's President Elect Ed Gunther led a discussion period which enabled members to share their feelings. IATC President Elect Tom Bird drove from Chicago to extend official greetings. IATC President Falconer tried to come from Akron, Ohio, to deliver that evening's Torch paper, but could not make the trip. Reed Taylor presided for Falconer.

Wright's sonnet commemorating Buffalo's 75th Anniversary was read. At Geneseo, New York, the first fall meeting, also planned for September 11, was rescheduled so as not to compete with prayer services at the State University College and in local churches.

July 1994-June 1995

Leadership included Acting President A. Reed Taylor and Executive Secretary and Treasurer James V. Strickland. (No separate treasurer was listed in the IATC Meeting Minutes for this decade; Jim Strickland presented the balance sheets and financial statements to the Board of Directors and at the General Business meetings.) At the start of the 1994 season, the elected president, Dean C. Gross from South Hampton Roads, Virginia, could neither start nor complete his term of office. Taylor assumed the role of acting president. He served as president from 1994-1997 without needing a replacement.

The IATC Board agreed to reduce the price of copies of *The Torch* to $7.50 for libraries. It was suggested that each club should purchase copies for their local library. If clubs wished to support two libraries with copies the local club would pay for the first subscription and the IATC would match the funds with a grant for the second library. Editor Patrick Dean shared the worksheets the reviewers used when considering articles for *The Torch.*

IATC membership stood at around 3,000 in 1994, with a total of seventy-nine clubs. The membership numbers were down slightly in 1995, with 2,848 members (a decline of 5 percent). It was also noted that many clubs still needed to submit their monthly reporting forms to their regional directors promptly. David Craig reported that a member of the Toronto Club did a presentation about Torch for the local Mensa Club. A St. Catharines, Ontario, Club member had friends in Toronto, he concluded, "so there is some hope there."

The IATC was carrying clubs in arrears for an extended length of time. Taylor encouraged the board to establish a firm policy setting a time limit for how long clubs in arrears would receive services. For example, support was provided to the Nashville, Tennessee, Club, which was in arrears by $2,200. The board forgave the debt. Taylor, Crepeau, Falconer, and Craig met with ten former club members. A reorganizational meeting was held; it was hoped that this would set the club on firmer ground.

The IATC convention was held in Detroit, Michigan, June 21-24. The board of directors initially met on June 21. One hundred and fifty-six members were in attendance for the entire convention.

The convention featured papers by Philip Mason ("Rum Running and the Roaring Twenties"), Harold Skramstad ("Detroit's Inventive Spirit, from Tom Edison to Motown"), Lucius Theus ("The Tuskegee Airmen—Pride and Prejudice"), Robert Cosgrove ("The New York Central and the Arts"), and Mary Kramer ("Take a Winner With You—Detroit and Windsor").

The Paxton Award was presented to Thomas L. Minnick. The Editor's Quill Award was presented to Walter J. Mueller of the Hampton Roads, Virginia, Club. One Gold and nine Silver

Torch Awards were presented. Clubs nominated for the Outstanding Torch Club Award included St. Catharines, Ontario (Region ; Trenton, New Jersey (Region ; Richmond, Virginia (Region 3); Athens, Georgia (Region 4); Akron, Ohio (Region 5); Detroit/Windsor, Detroit, Michigan, and Windsor, Ontario (Region 6); Lincoln, Nebraska (Region 7); and San Antonio, Texas (Region 9). The IATC recognized the Detroit/Windsor Club as the winner.

The reported balance of finances was $58,884.52 in checking. Bonds totaling either $28,000 or $29,000 (the minutes are unclear) had matured, and the board agreed to determine what amount would be invested in a Restricted Funds Investment account. The total dues receipts year-to-date were $89,863.75. The entire management expense was $22,320.57. The administrative expense was $19,244.63. Directors were encouraged to submit their reimbursements. The publication expenses totaled $26,000. Strickland predicted a slight surplus at the end of the year.

Latimer proposed a renumbering of the bylaws. His proposal inserted a new Section 8 (Charters) and renumbered the subsequent section as Section 9. The proposal contained five working points: requiring a club to send a written notice to the IATC stating the reason(s) for dissolution; requiring the IATC headquarters to send the notice to the IATC president, president elect, and the appropriate regional director; following a review by the executive committee and regional director, and after exploring all other alternatives, the item could be accepted and placed on the IATC Board agenda; upon acceptance by the IATC Board, the club was to be notified by letter of the decision, and the executive secretary would request the return of the original charter of the local club; each member of the dissolving club would be encouraged to retain their membership in Torch as a "member-at-large." The motion was approved.

Tours included the Henry Ford Museum, Greenfield Village, Detroit Institute of Arts, and the Cultural Center Museums.

July 1995-June 1996

Leadership included President A. Reed Taylor, President Elect Ruth E. Giller, and Executive Secretary and Treasurer James V. Strickland.

The board discussed the brochure "What Makes a Good Torch Paper?" Recommendations were made to make it more straightforward and reformulate the submission guidelines. Dean suggested a "Scoring System for Paxton Papers." Points to consider included the topic's contemporary significance, universality of interest, freshness, substance, provocative thesis, ability to lend itself to discussion or questions, ability to lend itself to oral delivery, organization, and presentation of a new topic or a novel approach to an old one.

A brainstorming memo by Craig and Crepeau included fourteen talking points. The comments ranged from discussing the running of board meetings to ways to increase participation by local membership. Notably, the memo suggested the need to rethink the matter of strong clubs helping weak clubs. Although it might seem that the strong clubs should be able to do something to assist the weak clubs in their vicinity, the strong clubs must continue to focus on actions that would keep their club strong. It was suggested that if a strong club could do some practical things to help a weak club without diminishing its strengths, the IATC should encourage it. The authors defined a weak club as those with nineteen or fewer members. The memo was followed up by further, largely supportive, reflection by Deans.

As of September 15, 1995, total IATC membership stood at 2,850, with memberships in seventy-eight clubs (not including the Nashville Club which was in arrears). The Dayton, Ohio, and Minneapolis, Minnesota, Clubs were struggling. No new clubs were recorded. The June 1996 membership report indicated a membership of 2,765, a decline of eighty-five members from the previous year. Seventy-eight clubs were in existence. The change in membership was dramatic enough that the membership committee was helping regional directors work with local clubs to revive their membership—this was referred to as "Regional Outreach." A suggestion was made by Falconer that "a club should be made more attractive to non-members and become more active." A new policy was formulated for new clubs and member development.

The 1996 Convention was held at the Desmond Hotel in Albany, New York, June 26-29. One hundred and fifty attendees were present for the entire convention.

Torch papers were presented by John W. Kalas ("The Role of Colleges and Universities in Preparing People for the Future"), Craig S. Williams ("The Impact of the Erie Canal on the Economy, Society, and Demographics of our Nation"), John McEneny ("The Rise and Fall of the Political Machine"), and George Wise ("Pioneering in Science and Technology in the Capital Region").

The Paxton awardee was Richard Schellhase. The Editor's Quill Award was presented to Pat Deans. Dick Lynch and George Crepeau were presented with Gold Torch Awards; eighteen Silver Torch Awards were presented.

The recommendations for the President's Award for Outstanding Torch Club included: Albany, New York (Region 1); Lancaster, Pennsylvania (Region 2); South Hampton Roads, Virginia (Region 3); Augusta, Georgia (Region 4); Columbia, South Carolina (Region 5), Saginaw Valley, Michigan (Region 6); Des Moines, Iowa (Region 7); and Houston, Texas (Region 9). The Award was given to the South Hampton Roads Club. The IATC also recognized Charles B. Hartley as an exemplary regional director, Fred Anderson as chairman of the finance committee, and David Craig with a special proclamation for spirited efforts in bringing another Canadian club into existence.

Strickland reported financial assets of $56,141.24. Year-to-date receipts totaled $90,039.50, and total disbursements were $68,100.01. Outstanding dues to be collected totaled $9,977.50.

The bylaws were amended to reflect several changes in policies. The changes addressed the process of selecting regional directors, appointed the president of the Torch Foundation as an *ex-officio* director on the IATC Board of Directors, provided for reimbursement of expenditures for IATC Board Committee members, and provided the board with the ability to create annual fees for members. The authority to conduct regular audits of the IATC books was also established. The motions were approved.

Attendees enjoyed guided tours of Albany and historic Lake George, the Schenectady Stockade Area, Union College's Nott Memorial Building, an operating canal lock, and scenic Saratoga (The Queen of American Spas).

July 1996-June 1997

Leadership included President A. Reed Taylor, President Elect Ruth E. Giller, and Executive Secretary and Treasurer James V. Strickland.

"The Torch Leader" was distributed to club presidents in 1997; the mailing contained postcards to be returned to maintain communication between IATC leadership and local clubs. Twelve of seventy-five clubs responded with postcards. There was a discussion of the value of the well-received "Torch Leader" and *The Torch* magazine as recruitment tools for membership. Suggestions were made about how to support recruitment efforts for new clubs and attract new members. Revision of the documents provided to authors continued. Bruce Souders revised the brochure "The Torch Paper Revisited."

At a board meeting, Peter Brown, a consultant, explained the World Wide Web and presented the benefits of having a web page on the network. Two of the advantages were that it would make the club visible to the public and create both a national and an international presence. Having a web address would allow the public to access information about the club. The cost estimate was determined to be between $1,500 and $4,000. Officers nominated for the committee on this issue were Leo Kellogg, Scott Stanfield, and Kate Fleischer.

Leo Kellogg (Saratoga, 2022)

The membership of IATC was 2,741 in February 1997, a decline of thirty-four from the previous year. The list of disbanded clubs included Syracuse, New York; Dayton, Ohio; and Raleigh,

North Carolina. Meeting notes indicated some turmoil in the Appleton, Wisconsin, Club which was receiving assistance from the regional director and other local clubs.

The 1997 Convention was held in the Radisson Hotel in Wilmington, Delaware, June 25-28. One hundred and thirty-nine members attended the full meeting.

Torch papers were presented by Gerald Christiansen ("Will Torch Go Bust As Boomers Age?"), Charles H. Holzinger ("The Promise of the Huan Genome Project: Blessing or Faustian Bargain?"), Ann Weller Dahl ("Laura Ingalls Wilder: Her Writing and Values Aren't Just for Children Anymore—and in Fact, Never Were"), and John C. Kraft ("The Preservation of Landscapes of the Past: Homer's Troy vs. Modern Development").

The Paxton Award winner was Leanne Wade Beorn. The Editor's Quill Awardee was Frank H. Callaham of South Hampton Roads, Virginia. A. Reed Taylor and Bruce Souders were recognized with Gold Torch Awards. Twenty Silver Torch Awards were presented. Clubs nominated by regional directors for recognition included St. Catharines, Ontario (Region 1); Wyoming Valley, Pennsylvania (Region 2); Winchester, Virginia (Region 3); Western South Carolina, South Carolina (Region 4); Toledo, Ohio (Region 5); Lansing, Michigan (Region 6); Des Moines, Iowa (Region 7); and Fort Worth, Texas (Region 9). Taylor presented the President's Award for the Outstanding Club to the Winchester Club.

Jim Strickland reported the IATC assets as $64,639.56. The year-to-date receipts were $90,200.85, and the total disbursements were $61,091.50. Outstanding receivables were at $8,096.50. Several clubs had outstanding balances but Strickland was confident that most of the dues would be quickly paid.

No bylaws amendments were proposed. Crepeau presented the Vision 2000+ Report entitled "A Vital Torch in the New Millennium." The report was divided into three sections: the Torch Concept, Torch Clubs, and the International Association of Torch Clubs. The report was a call to action urging the entire IATC membership to pursue this ongoing, transforming, strategic, and visionary plan.

Tours included Winterthur, the Hagley Museum, the Longwood Gardens, and the Brandywine River Museum.

July 1997-June 1998

Leadership included President Ruth Gillard, President Elect Ralph Falconer, and Executive Secretary and Treasurer James Strickland. Gail Strickland served as administrative assistant.

The need for an IATC website received additional discussion. It was noted that the Rochester Club had a strong website, but keeping it updated was a constant challenge. A motion was made and passed to authorize an IATC website. The cost for the establishment and operation of the website could not exceed $2,125. The website would be subject to the direction of the president or board of directors.

Anne Sterling, Ruth Giller, Ann Weller Dahl (IATC Presidents)

In June, the IATC membership stood at 2,728, representing seventy-five clubs.

However, the status of some clubs was uncertain. Individuals in the Gainesville, Florida, Club were on the rolls as at-large members. The Charlottesville, Virginia, Club was on the fence about retaining its membership; these club members were unaware of the benefits of being affiliated with the IATC. Reed Taylor agreed to visit the club and help them resolve their concerns. The Cumberland Valley, Pennsylvania, Club had dwindling membership and was considering disbanding.

The 1998 Convention was held in the Radisson Hotel, in Kalamazoo, Michigan, June 25-28. One hundred and fifty-nine members attended the full conference.

Papers were presented by Ralph Chandler ("The Idea of the City in Western Thought"), Jack Hopkins ("Energizing Solutions for Tomorrow's Communities"), and Kim Cummings ("Revitalizing the Local Community"). There was also a panel discussion by Nancy Arcadipone, Tom Huff, Nancy Troff, and Peter Weigand ("Adaptive Re-use of Urban Space").

Gerald G. Eggert won the Paxton Award. His paper, "The Professional," appeared in the Fall 1997 issue of *The Torch*. Deans recognized Lewis F. Russell from the San Antonio Club as winning of the Editor's Quill Award. Sixteen Silver Torch Awards were presented. Local clubs nominated for recognition included: Rochester, New York (Region 1); Central Pennsylvania, Pennsylvania (Region 2); Richmond, Virginia (Region 3); Columbia, South Carolina (Region 4); Butler County, Ohio (Region 5); Kalamazoo, Michigan (Region 6); Lincoln, Nebraska (Region 7);

and San Antonio, Texas (Region 9). The President's Award for Outstanding Club was given to the Central Pennsylvania Torch Club.

Strickland presented the most recent financial statement. Assets totaled $67,069.67. Year-to-date receipts totaled $91,097.31. Total disbursements were $62,174.42. Outstanding dues to be collected totaled $6,562.50.

Taylor extended an invitation to talk with clubs interested in hosting a convention. Giller encouraged the attendees to comment on whether scheduling the convention through Sunday was beneficial. Taylor addressed attracting new and younger members and commented on the necessity of meeting at an attractive location.

Falconer again expressed disappointment at the lack of growth in membership. There was a discussion about developing a membership pamphlet describing the qualifications of a good Torch member. A motion was made and tabled proposing the establishment of a Ben Franklin award to recognize growth in club membership and club development.

Tours included a walking tour of downtown Kalamazoo, a bus tour of historic homes, the Kalamazoo Nature Center, and the Gilmore Car Museum.

July 1998-June 1999

Leadership included President Ruth Gillard, President Elect Ralph Falconer, and Executive Secretary and Treasurer James Strickland. Gail Strickland served as administrative assistant.

The website again came up for discussion. Kellogg was working on ideas to get members to visit the IATC website. Suggestions included posting papers from *The Torch* and including links to local club websites. Fleisher and Stanfield were recognized for their contributions to the development and operation of the website from 1998 to 1999. Additionally, the IATC purchased an 800 telephone number and established an email address.

The Vision 2000+ Report by Crepeau was presented at an IATC board meeting. It was discussed, as were potential changes in the board, the executive committee, and the duties of the regional directors. Concern was expressed about whether the executive board members were elected or appointed solely by the president. Following extensive discussion, a motion to "accept in principle the Vision 2000+ Project" carried, and organizational changes were implemented.

The St. Catharines Club requested approval for acceptance of their membership dues in Canadian funds, due to the low exchange rate. On an annual basis, with their current membership of forty-one, they were paying $1,435 in US funds. In Canadian funds, this amount would be exchanged for $906.50, a difference of $528.50. A motion was made and carried to continue to set the budget by the US dollar, and the Canadian currency needed to be converted to US dollars.

The Columbia-Montour Club in Pennsylvania proposed to give a $500 scholarship to a student at Bloomsburg University. The board ruled that providing scholarships was not part of

Torch's mission, but the local club could provide the funds if the action was not identified with the IATC.

Paul Stanfield presented three drafts of the 1999-2000 budget in a May board meeting conference call. The first draft projected a decrease in income and expenses with no major changes, resulting in a deficit close to $10,000. The second draft showed an increase in dues of $5.00 a year to support the current expenditures. He did not recommend this option since many clubs had already set their dues for next year and might not want to make a change. The third draft included reducing expenditures by eliminating one of the newsletters, having an internal audit, and keeping *The Torch* its usual size. Another suggestion was to eliminate the newsletter as a separate publication, instead devoting space in the magazine to this purpose. A motion to adopt proposal three was made and carried. An additional motion was made to propose a $5.00 dues increase for the 2000-2001 year; this would be voted on at the Toledo Convention.

Club membership in 1999 decreased to 2,582, a decline from the previous year of eighty-six. There were 196 new members. The number of clubs held steady at seventy-five. The Gainesville, Florida, and Cumberland Valley, Pennsylvania, Clubs struggled. Kellogg recorded an interview with Allan Powell discussing starting new clubs; this tool would become available to local clubs looking for guidance.

The 1999 Convention was held at the Radisson Hotel in Toledo, Ohio, June 24-27. One hundred and twenty-one members attended the full conference.

Papers were presented by David C. Skaggs ("The Sixty Year Struggle for the Great Lakes") and Elliot J. Tramer ("Erie: Rebirth of a Great Lake"). A panel discussion was presented by Edward F. Weber, Dick Anderson, Glen Hiner, Edward Teiter, and Norman Thal ("Northwest Ohio: From Rust Belt to Boom Belt").

Mary Frances Forcier won the Paxton Award. The Editor's Quill Award winner was Christopher H. Hodgman from the Rochester Club. This year, there were two Gold Torch Award recipients: May Alice Butkofski of the Lancaster, Pennsylvania, Club and John A. Mapp of the Richmond, Virginia, Club. Seventeen Silver Torch Awards were also given.

Regional directors recommended the following clubs for recognition: Elmira, New York (Region 1); Gettysburg-Adams, Pennsylvania (Region 2); Hagerstown, Maryland (Region 3); Athens, Georgia (Region 4); Columbus, Ohio (Region 5); Saginaw Valley, Michigan (Region 6); Lincoln, Nebraska (Region 7); and Houston, Texas (Region 9). The Hagerstown Torch Club was awarded the Presidential Award for the Outstanding Torch Club.

Strickland presented the financial statement. Assets totaled $69,163.94, receipts totaled $82,059.66, and total disbursements were $63,043.07. Outstanding dues totaled $9,817.50. He distributed the proposed 1999-2000 budget. A $5.00 increase per member would be the first since 1989.

Kellogg presented the following plan for a membership development project that included the following points: ask local clubs to designate a person to communicate with IATC concerning membership development, write a membership development function statement for club designees and send it to all club presidents, update and redistribute the "Torch International Membership Development Handbook," include monthly updates via the "Torch Leader" monthly newsletter, encourage every region to establish at least one new Torch Club this year, ask all Torch Clubs for examples of effective membership development, visit selected Torch Clubs to discuss membership development, place the "IATC Membership Development Handbook" on the IATC website, and research what other organizations do to encourage membership.

Marshall Giller and Jack Whyte provided an entertaining and welcoming song entitled "Viva Toledo." Tours included the Toledo Museum of Art, the Old West End Historic District, Maumee Bay Maritime Cruise, the Erie Street Market, and the Toledo Zoo.

July 1999-June 2000

Leadership included President Ralph C. Falconer, President Elect Thomas J. Bird, and Executive Secretary and Treasurer James V. Strickland. Gail Strickland served as the executive assistant.

Leo Kellogg submitted a report on computer communications to the fall board meeting. A major upgrade of the "Torch Directory" on the IATC website was done in February of 2000. New functions included ability to search for clubs by name, city, state, or region. Contact information for the officers of each club was shown, as well as a list of current members. Links were also provided to websites maintained by local clubs. The latest issues of *The Torch* and *The Torchlight* were also added to the website's publications section. Images of the documents were created entirely electronically, a novel idea at the time. The IATC also invested in Livestats, a cutting-edge software tool used to collect website usage statistics. Suggestions for further enhancements included a chat room, posting of unpublished Torch papers, and an index of Torch papers by name and date for every Torch Club that wished to provide that listing.

Deans encouraged everyone to continue sending quality papers for publication in *The Torch*, which was expanded to thirty-six pages to allow for more articles.

The "Torch Leader" published profiles of local clubs which were well received. A recommendation was made to include a copy of the "Torch Leader" in new club packets.

Regional director's reports were filed. A particularly poignant note appeared regarding the Jamestown Torch Club. Wilber H. Wright, the Region 1 Director, wrote: "I visited with the Jamestown officers on July 30, 1999. The club is to be commended for still existing with six members paying dues. All are past presidents. Two are in their 80s, and four are in their 70s. The president for the last 14 years writes, 'The inevitable demise of our club, like our members, can occur anytime.'"

Strickland reported the membership was 2,554 as of May 31. There was a decline of twenty-eight members from a year earlier. Two hundred seventy-three new members were added during the current year. Four clubs disbanded, including Cumberland Valley, Pennsylvania; Gainesville, Florida; Heartland, Florida; and Central Texas. New clubs included Fox Valley, Wisconsin, and Waynesboro, Pennsylvania. There were seventy-three Torch Clubs in existence.

The 2000 Convention was held at Shenandoah University in Winchester, Virginia, June 22-25. One hundred and fifty-one attendees participated in the full conference.

Papers presented included "The Frontier Meets the Youth, and Vice Versa," "Did Richard Byrd Fly Over the North Pole?," and "Willa Cather: Local Girl to Literary Classic."

The Paxton Award winner was Robert G. Neuhauser from the Lancaster, Pennsylvania, Club. Gold Torch Awards were presented to R. Patrick Deans (South Hampton Roads, Virginia), Ruth E. Giller (Grand Rapids, Michigan), and Edward B. Latimer (Columbia, South Carolina). Seventeen Silver Torch Awards were presented.

The following clubs were recommended for recognition: Buffalo, New York (Region 1); Wilmington, Delaware (Region 2); Winchester, Virginia (Region 3); Boca Raton, Florida (Region 4); Columbus, Ohio (Region 5); Grand Rapids, Michigan (Region 6); Des Moines, Iowa (Region 7); and San Antonio, Texas (Region 9). The Columbus Club was awarded the President's Outstanding Club Award for 2000.

Strickland presented the financial report. Assets totaled $80,236.75. Receipts to date were $86,967.14. Total disbursements were $61,360.83. Excess receipts over disbursements totaled $25,606.31.

There was a discussion of the bylaws regarding the Silver Torch Awards and the Regional and Presidential Awards.

Kellogg suggested that when both a husband and wife were members of a Torch Club, a reduction in the IATC membership fee be made. The fee might be $40 less (the cost of *The Torch*). For a spouse incentive, Wilbur Wright proposed that one-half ($20) of the annual IATC dues be offered as a one-time credit.

A motion was made and carried to amend guidelines for how convention profits were allocated. Under the new guidelines profits of up to $5,000 would be shared equally between the host club and the IATC. Monies collected over that amount would go to the IATC. It was directed that the first $1,000 surplus received by the IATC would be deposited in the Convention Reserve Fund.

July 2000-June 2001

Leadership remained the same as in 1999-2000: President Ralph Falconer, President Elect Thomas J. Bird, and Executive Secretary and Treasurer James V. Strickland. Gail Strickland served as the executive assistant.

In a March 22 meeting, Falconer proposed to meet with the Columbus Club in April and ask them to form a task force to gather information on all the papers presented in *The Torch*. Once this information was collected a library could be established where distribution of the papers could be granted for a small fee. A motion to this effect was made and carried.

Linda Porter and Ralph Falconer

The "Regional Director's Report," dated January 19, 2001, carried an interesting account by Bill Estran of Region 3. He visited clubs in Washington, DC; Frederick, Maryland; Durham-Chapel Hill, North Carolina; Winston-Salem, North Carolina; Montgomery County, Alabama; Portsmouth, New Hampshire; Winchester, Virginia; and San Antonio, Texas. He had a disappointing experience at the Chapel Hill Club. The two most influential members organized a movement to withdraw from the IATC. When he arrived late at the president's home, the club had already voted eight-to-one to withdraw. He asked the members three questions: (1) How many conventions had they been to? (2) How much of *The Torch* did they read, and how many papers had they submitted? (3) How much had they used the website? The answers were mostly negative. Then he asked how long they thought the club would last without the affiliation. That reversed the vote to eight-to-one to maintain association with the IATC.

Strickland reported Torch membership of 2,557 as of June 2000, in seventy-four clubs. The 262 new members led to a net increase of three overall. A new club was chartered in Geneseo, New York with twenty-nine members and a woman president.

The 2001 Convention was held at the White Oaks Conference Resort, Niagara-on-the-Lake, Ontario, Canada. One hundred and forty-nine attendees participated in the full convention.

Papers were presented by Patricia Dirks, ("Et le Québec?"), Larry Tokarchuk ("How Canada's Health System Works"), and Ian J. Roland ("Professional Self-Governance in the Canadian

Legal Context"). A panel was presented by Laura Bruce, Milica Kovacevich, and Doug Rapelje ("Nonprofits and Public Entrepreneurship in Canada").

Jonathon B. Wight of Richmond, Virginia, won the Paxton Award for his paper "A Little Adam Smith is a Dangerous Thing." Peter G. Mowitt of Winchester, Virginia, was recognized with the Editor's Quill Award for his paper "Daniel Morgan: The King of Battletown." Gold Torch Awards were presented to David Craig, St. Catharines, Ontario; Leo A. Kellogg, Albany, New York; and Wilbur H. Wright, Rochester, New York. Twenty-four Silver Torch Awards were also presented.

The following clubs were recognized by their regional directors: St. Catharines, Ontario (Region 1); Reading, Pennsylvania (Region 2); South Hampton Roads, Virginia (Region 3); Columbia, South Carolina (Region 4); Toledo, Ohio (Region 5); Grand Rapids, Michigan (Region 6); Boulder, Colorado (Region 7); Fort Worth, Texas (Region 9). The St. Catharines Club received the President's Outstanding Club Award.

Strickland presented the financial report. Year-to-date receipts were $94,418.64, disbursements were $72,956.20. The excess of receipts over disbursements was $21,462.64. The current assets totaled $81,288.80.

Falconer proposed that the IATC offer up to $500 to organizers of new Torch Clubs. The IATC would send serious inquiries $100 to start, $200 when ten members signed up, and another $200 when they acquired twenty or more members (enough to charter a club). The motion was made and carried.

Tours included Niagara Falls and the Niagara Parkway, the Welland Canal, a winery and orchards, lunch at the Table Rock Restaurant, and lunch at the Freighters Food Emporium.

July 2001-June 2002

Leadership remained unchanged: President Ralph Falconer, President Elect Thomas J. Bird, and Executive Secretary and Treasurer James V. Strickland. Gail Strickland served as the executive assistant.

David Smith contacted Editor Deans about creating a library of Torch papers. Deans offered to contact authors and request a synopsis of their work. The papers could be copied and sent to the archives along with the synopsis. Smith said that once this was implemented available papers would be listed on the Torch website. Most papers he received were digital and could be sent online. A suggestion was also made to start a newsletter competition; Joe Smith suggested that this would be a way to expand local clubs' monthly newsletters and to improve their quality.

Falconer reviewed a proposal to develop a past president's pin. He continued to work on this project.

Strickland reported that the total Torch membership was 2,554 in May of 2002. There was a loss of 301 members, with 273 new members joining clubs, for a net decline of thirty-eight. There was also a loss of three clubs: Cumberland Valley, Pennsylvania; Gainesville, Florida; and Central Texas. New clubs were chartered in Waynesboro, Pennsylvania; Fox Valley, Wisconsin; and Adirondack, New York. Strickland observed that the IATC was losing about 10 percent of its members yearly due to resignations, relocations, and deaths. Bird suggested acknowledging the loss of a member due to relocation to a nursing home or death with a postcard from Torch International.

The 2002 Convention was held in Athens, Georgia, June 27-30. One hundred and five members were registered for the full convention.

Papers were presented by Corrie Brown ("Future Shock: Bio- and Agro-terrorism"), Cliff Baile ("Rapidly Growing Field of Agricultural Biotechnology—A Glance at the Past and a Vision for the Future"), Charles Hudson ("Conversations with the High Priest of Coosa"), Daniel Colley ("The Global Challenge of Emerging and Re-emerging Infectious Diseases"), and James Cobb ("Dixie International: The South and the Global Econo-Culture").

Strickland presented the financial report. Year-to-date receipts were $97,057.78 and disbursements were $68,401.34. Excess receipts over disbursements were $28,656.44. Current assets totaled $87,369.60.

Falconer proposed a change in the bylaws to allow for discounted IATC dues for the Canadian clubs. Following much discussion, this motion was made and carried: "The annual IATC dues for Torch Clubs outside the United States shall be paid in US dollars and shall be equal to one-half the difference between the US dollars and the local currency according to the rate of exchange on October 1 and March 1."

July 2002-June 2003

Leadership included President Tom Bird, President Elect Wayne M. Davis, and Executive Secretary and Treasurer James Strickland. Gail Strickland remained as the Executive Assistant.

Deans, in his editor's report, presented the 2003-2004 publication schedule which included the name of the publication (*The Torch* or *The Torchlight*) and the deadlines for "materials," "materials to the typist," "copy to the editor," "copy to the printer," "copy to the mailer," and the date the materials were to be delivered to the Post Office. (While this level of organization was impressive, it is a relief to know that we are no longer relying on typists to prepare clean copies of our texts!) It was reported by Deans that there was a better flow of high-quality papers than in the past. *The Torch* was being actively used as a recruitment tool.

A motion was approved at the IATC board meeting to reduce the Silver Torch Award recognition qualifications from ten to five years of membership.

The Adirondack, Ohio, Torch Club was chartered May 2. Stan Burdick started the club. He was a member of the Firelands/Sandusky, Ohio, Torch Club for seven years. The $500 subsidy from the IATC enabled him to recruit thirty-four new members. Fifty-five people attended the chartering meeting. Strickland reported a membership of 2,536 as of June 1. This total indicated a decline of forty-one members from 2002, and a total of 234 new members. Meanwhile the Jamestown, New York, Club dissolved.

At the Chicago 2003 Convention papers were presented by Earl C. Swallow ("Science, Pseudoscience and Self-Deception"), Isaac Bloom ("Green Communities"), David R. Baier ("Great Lakes: Past, Present and Future"), James E. Lindell ("Deep Tunnel: Looking Forward, Looking Backward"), and David E. Barclay ("The View from Elgin, Illinois: Stereotypes in German-American Relations").

The Paxton Award winner was Mark Lore from the Winchester, Virginia, Club, for his paper "Can War Be Rational? How Do Nations Get Their Way?" This was a stellar year for awards, with Gold Awards given to three members: Charles Greeb, Jr., Winchester, Virginia; Allan Powell, Hagerstown, Maryland; and William Troxell, Richmond, Virginia. Twenty Silver Torch Awards were presented.

Concerns were raised about the number of registrations for the 2003 Chicago Convention, which stood at 121. At the board meeting prior to the convention, Stephen Toy presented the following data on annual convention attendance:

Convention	Year	Total Registrants	Whole Registrations*
Chicago, IL	2003	121	
Athens, GA	2002	153	105
St. Catharines, CA	2001	181	149
Winchester, VA	2000	178	
Toledo, OH	1999	170	121
Kalamazoo, MI	1998	171	133
Wilmington, DE	1997	145	139
Albany, NY	1996	178	150
Detroit, MI	1995	168	156
Norfolk, VA	1994	138	N/A

*Please note: "Whole Registrations" references Torch Club members and/or representatives who attended all business meetings and activities. "Total Registrants" includes the "Whole Registrations" and spouses and significant others who attended many, if not all, convention sessions.

Strickland presented the financial report. Year-to-date receipts were $97,688.59. Disbursements were $71,039.98. Excess receipts over disbursements were $26,648.61. Current assets totaled $89,896.60.

Leadership included President Tom Bird, President Elect Wayne M. Davis, and Executive Secretary and Treasurer James V. Strickland. Gail Strickland served as the executive assistant.

Monthly club reports, order forms, membership applications, and manuscript submission forms were added to the IATC website.

Region 3 had grown quite large, with a total of fifteen clubs. Bird proposed restructuring Region 3 into two regions—the northern half (Washington, Baltimore, Frederick, Hagerstown, Tri-state/Cumberland, Winchester, and West Virginia), and making Region 8 the southern half (Durham-Chapel Hill, Winston-Salem, Hampton Roads, Virginia, Montgomery County, Alabama, Portsmouth, Virginia, Richmond, Virginia, Roanoke Valley, Virginia, and South Hampton Roads, Virginia).

Wayne Davis (IATC President), Anne Sterling (IATC President Elect),
Thomas Bird (IATC Immediate Past President)

Membership was 2,485 as of June 1, 2004. Forty-nine members were lost from the previous year, while 207 were added. The Detroit/Windsor and Minneapolis Clubs disbanded. New clubs included: Asheville, North Carolina; Fredericksburg, Virginia; and Chambersburg, Pennsylvania. The fledgling club in Asheville had thirteen deposits and ninety potential members as of May 2004. The board agreed to award a $500 grant to Allan Powell for the establishment of the new Chambersburg Club.

The 2004 Convention was held in Wilkes-Barre, Pennsylvania, June 24-27.

Papers were presented by Michael Knies ("The Anthracite Region of Northeast Pennsylvania"), Christopher Brieseth ("The Wyoming Valley: An Historical Perspective"), William S.

Pierce ("New Help for Failing Hearts: Progress and Promise"), and Jane Elmes-Crahall ("Controlling Spin: News, Politics and PR").

The Paxton Award winner was Matthew T. Taylor, Sr. The IATC recognized two Torch members with Gold Torch Awards: Gilles O. Allard (Athens, Georgia), and William E. Elstan (Durham-Chapel Hill, North Carolina). Elstan's award was made posthumously. Fourteen Silver Torch Awards were also presented.

Strickland presented the financial report. Year-to-date receipts were $99,382.23 and disbursements were $71,326.63. Excess receipts over disbursements were $28,055.60. Current assets totaled $97,383.16. A balanced budget was expected at year's end. Outstanding receivables totaled $2,580.

Spousal membership had turned a corner. Now, with the acceptance of women into Torch, there was a proposal by Charles Carlson to eliminate dues on the international or club level for the spouses of paying members. Following discussion, the suggestion was made to consider establishing a lower fee for spouses to attend the dinner meeting.

The IATC Bylaws were amended, changing minimum qualifications and terms set for the president, president elect, and all directors. Concerns were raised about the voting method for the nomination of a president elect. At the time, each club had one vote but sent two delegates to vote at the convention. It was decided that each club would have only one vote and submit a written ballot. It was also decided to display the three most recent editions of *The Torch* on the website.

Tours included the Lackawanna Coal Mine, Ricketts Glen State Park, Historic Wyoming Valley, Eckley Miners Village, Frances Slocum State Park, and Steam Town National Historic Site.

Ann Weller Dahl, Leo McPherson (Silver Torch Award), Janet Henry (Baltimore Torch)

Chapter 4: July 2004-June 2014

Written by John Tordiff
Researched by Rich Davis and Diane Selby

Decade Overview

July 2004 to June 2014 was another decade of declining membership and disappearing clubs for all the reasons mentioned in earlier chapters. Again this decade the IATC was fortunate to have a series of talented and motivated presidents who, together with fellow board members, had a positive plan of how the membership issue could be addressed. The IATC's leadership was a collective effort by a geographically diverse and professionally eclectic group. While the IATC President set the tone and spotlighted specific issues, it was the joint decisions of the IATC Board of Directors (hereafter, the board) that established the boundaries, directed the expenditures of money, undertook informational studies, and planned for the future of the organization. It is important, therefore, to identify who was in this band of leaders, how they tried to remain consistent, and what actions they authorized for the betterment of the IATC. Also, this chapter will chronicle the conventions and the continuing efforts to strengthen Torch by the head office administrators, *The Torch* editors, the Torch Foundation officers and directors, and by unexpected new leaders emerging from the club membership. Not all notable Torch leaders can be mentioned, but a representative sample will demonstrate the skill and dedication commonplace among board members. This chapter will illustrate, often in their own words, what the board members were thinking and how they envisioned the common effort. Declining membership was a struggle. The statistics were available. The trend was obvious. But how to combat it? Beyond the board, who were the people involved in the effort? How did they approach the problem? What resources were marshaled? What successes did they have? What obstacles did they meet? What corrective measures did they implement? In short, what happened?

Among the remarkable leaders in this decade were Allen and Joanie Powell, an amazing couple who recruited the equivalent of an entire IATC Region. Allen had been a teacher for forty-one years, completing his career as a professor at Hagerstown Community College. He wrote six books on the French-Indian War period and one book on theology. He wrote extensively for *The Torch*, both as an IATC official and also as the author of "Appearance vs Reality: Plato's Problem—Our Problem." He substituted for President Toy with an inspiring column entitled "Another Torch Convention—Another Renewed Spirit." Joanie Powell must have been inspired by her husband because together they are believed to have sponsored, founded, revived, or mentored eight Torch Clubs—the equivalent of a Powell family Torch region! President Anne Sterling was profuse in her praise of this couple: "Allan and his wife Joanie are delightful to work with." While Sterling was co-director of Region 3 the Powell recruitment blitz made the region so large that it forced a multi-region realignment. Allan Powell joined the board under President Wayne Davis and became Member-at-Large for

Membership. He led workshops and wrote pamphlets and articles on membership recruitment. In tribute, President Sterling said "Allan Powell is a folk hero within our organization, having founded numerous clubs." He resigned in May 2010. The board offered him an honorary life membership but he modestly and gracefully declined the honor.

Joanie and Allan Powell

Another remarkable couple were Jimmy and Gail Strickland who retired after careers as IATC administrators spanning 1995 to 2010. As mentioned in the previous chapter, the Stricklands operated a small "mom and pop" accounting firm in Norfolk, Virginia. They became the IATC's management team for the next sixteen years. Jimmy was the new executive secretary and chief accountant. Gail was the office manager, liaison, and file keeper. Gail's cheery Southern accent and sunny attitude brightened many a mundane administrative long-distance telephone conversation. For the first three years they worked closely with President Reed Taylor to learn the rhythm and routines of the organization. Quickly they were welcomed into the Torch family. Their efforts were acknowledged by President Sterling:

> Board efforts (to cut costs) were echoed in our Torch Office, in Virginia. There Jimmy and Gale Strickland kept up their outstanding—even expanding—service to Clubs. Yet the bills they submitted did not increase over earlier years. Like the baker who throws in an extra doughnut or two they found ingenious ways to save, and let Torch become the beneficiary of their efforts.

Upon their retirement on June 30, 2010, Jimmy Strickland commented, "We have managed Torch with the same values we have managed our firm: with honesty, integrity and commitment."

Before delving into a detailed examination of annual events, here is a "big picture" overview of the decade. In June 2004 there were 2,488 Torch Club members organized into seventy-one clubs. There was one international club, in Canada. By June 2014 there were 2,190 members in sixty-seven clubs with the lone Canadian club persisting. During the decade twelve clubs dissolved, but nine new clubs emerged. Membership had slowly declined each year except for a brief positive bounce to 2,444 members in 2007. As a result of an earlier bylaw ruling, the criteria for membership had been delegated to the discretion of local clubs. No statistics were kept by the IATC on the local definition of "professional," the number of female members, or the participation of minorities. Nevertheless, a significant sign that positive changes were happening was the appearance of female leaders at both the international and club levels. Ruth Giller of the Grand Rapids, Michigan, Club was IATC President 1997-1999, followed by Anne Sterling 2005-2007. More and more IATC Directors were women—two on the 2004-2005 Board and three on the 2012-2013 Board. By way of a typical example of a female club executive, the St. Catharines Club elected Presidents H. Irene Kadongag 1988-1989, Luzviminda G. Reyes 1990-1991, Mollinda Alexson 2002-2003, and Cecilia W. C. Yau 2003-2004. Similarly, distinguished St. Catharines Club members from visible minorities were Thilagavathi (Tilly) Chandulal, Selvum Pillay, and the inestimable Eknath Marathe. At this point it would seem relevant given the above references to the activities of a Canadian club to briefly address the "International" part of the International Association of Torch Clubs.

The International Aspect of the IATC

The IATC sought to have an international presence from the very beginning. It was not until 1937—thirteen years into IATC's existence and thanks to the efforts of the Buffalo Torch Club—that the first international Torch affiliate was founded in Hamilton, Ontario, Canada. All nine subsequent Canadian clubs were formed in the Canadian province of Ontario. The Hamilton Club went on to provide two IATC presidents, F. R. Murgatroyd 1946-1947 and C. H. Stearn 1953-1954. In 1947 Hamilton was the host of the first convention held outside of the United States. There were two more Canadian IATC Presidents, Edward M. Shortt of the London, Ontario, Club 1959-1960 and Edgar T. Peer of the St. Catharines Club 1967-1968. On April 5, 1975, a promising total of five Canadian clubs met for a regional mini-convention in Hamilton, Ontario. The nine clubs were never in existence simultaneously.

Canada was not the only country targeted for potential Torch expansion clubs. Board of Directors Minutes for April 1983 suggested contacting embassies in Washington, DC, to explore interest in new clubs abroad. Additional feelers were put out for possible clubs in Monterey, Mexico, in 1983 and London, England, in 1984.

Meanwhile, the five Canadian clubs of 1975 had shrunk by 1979 to Windsor, St. Catharines, and Kitchener-Waterloo. There were still three clubs in 1983 but these gradually dwindled to a single Canadian Club, St. Catharines, by 2004. In spite of its lonely status, St. Catharines hosted conventions in 2001 and 2014.

Are there unique issues which have led to the decline of the Canadian wing of Torch International? The general trend away from public participation in community special-purpose clubs is not clearly evident in Canada. New-approach clubs such as The Third Age Learning Network and Probus Clubs have continued to prosper. So the causes must lie elsewhere. The need to make purchases and pay dues in US dollars discouraged Canadian members. In the heady days of the 1950s the two currencies were almost even, but by the 2000s the exchange rate required a 10 to 35 percent surcharge on converting Canadian membership fees into US dollars. Next, there are the cultural nuances that had some Canadian members suggesting that too many articles in *The Torch* are "American-centric." This bias was understandable given that Canadian clubs represented only 1 or 2 percent of the total number. It is worth noting that clubs from different nations are going to feel the emotional tug to have the story told from their own perspective. In fairness, the IATC leadership and *The Torch* editors in particular have been generous and supportive in praising and publishing Canadian contributions. The St. Catharines Club alone has had over thirty articles printed in *The Torch*. Finally, with declining membership, the club leadership and the speaker pool became less vital. And so competing venues, punishing exchange rates, national sensitivities, and shrinking membership all played their part in dwindling participation.

A Decade of Hope

The goals of the IATC leadership and of the constituent member clubs have always remained the same—to grow Torch with more clubs and more members while maintaining the commendable standards and honorable values of Torch. Each president had a significantly different approach to solving the problem of declining membership. President Wayne Davis decided on an intellectual appeal to the club leadership, while simultaneously collaborating with Allan Powell's club-generating genius. President Anne Sterling used personal contact through extensive travel to build bonds, to recruit talent, and to create a comfortable fellowship of leaders and members. President Stephen Toy tackled the looming financial crisis brought on by membership decline. It was a thankless job, but it won Torch several years of stability and program growth. His solid logic and obvious love of Torch set a worthy example. President Edward Latimer exhibited folksy charm combined with vast experience in Torch. His was another period of leadership stability. The decade was completed by President Charles Carlson who brought organizational genius and forward-looking thinking to the membership fight. He organized coordinated actions by all available resources on all available fronts and he expedited the adoption of modern communication technologies. June 2014 was an optimistic moment in IATC history thanks to the efforts of these five leaders and their teams of supporters.

While not as high-profile as the elected leadership, IATC was fortunate to have stable and competent administrators through most of this decade. They were, in retrospect, somewhat handicapped by the primitive accounting and membership tracking techniques. This does not reflect poorly on them since they were working with the technology available at the time. Later efforts to streamline and modernize the membership tracking process met with delay and confusion because of a computer subcontractor's failure to complete the transfer of written files to electronic records. Beginning in 2013 it took a heroic effort on the part of Jim Coppinger and Mark Dahmke to untangle and reorganize Torch's administrative records.

During this decade of technological change *The Torch* remained the premier IATC publication, providing a steady stream of interesting, thoughtful, and informative articles by Torch scholars. Numerous changes were made to cut costs yet improve the look and professional aura of the magazine. It wasn't the only publication that the skillful IATC team provided to the membership. *The Torchlight* electronic bulletin took on the role of internal organizational newsletter, providing news on significant personnel changes, club events, and administrative timetables. It offered the occasional advice column on membership retention or growth. The "Torch Leader" was an occasional printed bulletin sent to club executives to provide advice and to offer news pertinent to a club's leadership. Lastly, the IATC website went through several trials and modifications on its way to eventually becoming a modern, easily accessible source of information and communication for all Torch members.

July 2004-June 2005

Wayne M. Davis was elected IATC President at the Wyoming Valley Convention in Wilkes Barre, Pennsylvania, June 24-27, 2004. The Board of Directors consisted of President Elect Anne Sterling, Immediate Past President Thomas J. Bird, Directors Charles E. Carlson (Region 1), John B. Cornish (Region 2), Ann Weller Dahl (Region 3), Edward B. Latimer (Region 4), John A. Horner, Jr. (Region 5), Jack C. Jones (Region 6), John Fowler (Region 7), Matthew T. Taylor (Region 8), Ernest A. Lantz (Region 9), David C. Smith (Director-at-Large, Membership), Stephen T. Toy (Director-at-Large, Conventions), and Torch Foundation President Ralph C. Falconer. Administrative support consisted of Executive Secretary James V. Strickland, Jr. and Editor R. Patrick Deans.

Club leadership development was the theme of Davis's presidency. In his initial communication to local Torch Club presidents he warned that "your greatest problem will be maintaining membership." Experience, he warned, showed that clubs normally lost 10 percent of their members every year. He urged that each club set a goal of recruiting two new members or 10 percent of membership. He also mentioned the possibility of establishing a leadership college or institute.

At the 2004 Convention a number of important initiatives and recommendations were passed, including Bird and Falconer's *Election Manual*, Smith's "Recruiting and Retaining Members" resource guide, extensive bylaw amendments related to election procedures, and a change of Foundation leadership from George Crepeau to Ralph Falconer. It fell to Davis and his team to act on these changes.

To streamline the timing of convention events *The Torch* Editor Deans proposed limiting the Paxton winning essay to 3,000 words, reducing presentation time to a comfortable thirty minutes. His proposal was accepted. Then Deans asked the board if a paper by Robert G. Neuhauser, "Toward a New Feudal Society," should be published "since there is so much controversy with it." Neuhauser, a devout Quaker, offered an eloquent and heartfelt interpretation of European and American history which suggested that a powerful minority consisting of the wealthy, the church, and the military cooperated to control national politics and the economy to the disadvantage of the majority of citizens. The board opted to approve publishing the article.

Ann Weller Dahl and Anne Sterling (2004, 2023)

To enhance communication between the IATC and the clubs, regional directors were encouraged to produce regional newsletters. One such document was the "Region One Mid-Winter Newsletter" of 2004-2005 written by Carlson. In it, he mentioned that the IATC website was a source of information about the 2005 Convention in Des Moines, that two Region 1 clubs had their own websites, and offered some thoughts about membership development from Abel Fink of the Buffalo Club and Harold Rubin of the Albany Club. In addition, he gave a breakdown of where the IATC dues were spent; for example 31 percent went to publications such as *The Torch*, *The Torchlight*, and the "Officers Directory." Finally, Carlson explained that the Torch Foundation was an independent legal entity with a separate board of directors and a separate budget that worked in cooperation with the IATC. Its major expense was the Paxton Lecture's $500 cash award.

Given growing confidence in the work of Executive Secretary Strickland and his team, the temporary position of Torch Secretary, which had been so capably filled by Dick Lynch, was deemed unneeded and phased out. The Finance Committee consisting of Chair George Heron, Lynch, and Falconer took on the task of creating an investment policy for IATC's assets and preparing an investment proposal for those assets. The History Committee of Chair Arthur Goldschmidt, Abel Fink, and Keir Sterling was charged with writing an update of Torch's history. By way of encouragement for this effort, the Torch Foundation allotted $1,275. An *ad hoc* committee from Athens, Georgia, undertook to prepare a membership recruitment DVD. The committee included Gilles Allard, President Elect Sterling, Latimer, and Leo Kellogg.

Strickland, in his Executive Secretary's Report, praised the Torch emblem. Quoting an unnamed source he said,

> The purpose of the Torch emblem is to blaze the way with light and truth
> to a greater fraternal spirit among professional men in service to society.
> The triangle represents three of the great branches of professional activity: science, literature and art. The Torch motto is "*True Service to Society through the Professions.*"

In a moment of impressive optimism or administrative zeal, or perhaps frustrated mischievousness, the board passed a bylaw amendment creating a new section entitled "dissolution procedure for clubs." This protocol required dying or deceased clubs to send in a formal notification announcing their intention to expire shortly or their expectation of staying expired. This is proof that the board had either great expectations or a wry sense of humor or, most likely, both.

On a more prosaic matter, there was a formal designation of the standing IATC committees: (1) Awards, (2) Bylaws/Constitution, (3) Convention, (4) Finance/Budget, (5) Membership, (6) Nominations, and (7) Website. Copies of a DVD on membership development created by David Smith would be sold for $10 each at the next convention.

The Association's Financial Statements for the Fiscal Year ending June 30, 2005 showed income of $97,276.41 with expenses of $101,298.03 for a net deficit of $4,021.62. Total assets were $69,827.69. Not a good sign.

Sadly, the Champaign County, Illinois, Torch Club was dissolved on October 25, 2004. In happier news, Allan Powell, in his role as Director-at-Large for Membership, helped charter the Asheville-Blue Ridge, North Carolina, Club on April 6, 2005 and successfully revived the Chambersburg, Pennsylvania, Club on April 11, 2005. Spring 2005 saw a realignment of Torch Club regions spearheaded by Sterling and Dahl. Thanks in part to the recruiting efforts of Allan and Joanie Powell, Region 3 had become cumbersome with sixteen clubs, so a new "I-81 corridor" grouping was created by pulling clubs from Regions 2 and 3. This reorganization meant that there were now seven clubs in Region 2, six clubs in Region 3, and eight clubs in the newly designated Region 8.

The 2005 Convention in Iowa, titled "Des Moines. The Surprising Place!" was held June 23 26. "Our goal is to surprise, delight, entertain, challenge, and excite IATC Convention guests." Attendance was 133, slightly down from 142 at Wilkes-Barre in 2004. The decrease was attributed to the farther traveling distance and added costs to delegates from the East Coast.

The 2005 Paxton Award went to Robert G. Neuhauser for "Toward a New Feudal Society." The Editor's Quill Award 2005 went to Joseph Calderone of Elmira, New York, for his article "Wine and Health." Gold Torch Awards went to Bird of the Chicago Club, Toy of the Delaware Club, and Smith of the Western Maine Club. Also, fifteen Silver Torch Awards were issued. The recipient of the Outstanding Club Award 2005 was not recorded.

Attendees were treated to a special "Passport to Iowa" dinner featuring menu items brought to Iowa by immigrant populations. Generally the tours had an informative agricultural, wildlife, or governmental structures theme. Many delegates were pleasantly shocked by a presentation entitled "The Iowa Great Ape Trust" and by a staging of "The Tales of Hoffman" by the Des Moines Metropolitan Opera.

July 2005-June 2006

Directors serve a two-year term with half the directors rotating out at every annual general business meeting to provide continuity. Newly elected directors in June 2006 were Linda Porter (Region 5), George R. Heron (Region 6), Arthur F. Dawes, III (acting director Region 9), and John A. Horner (Director-at Large, Conventions).

In his second year as president, Davis addressed the issue of declining membership in *The Torch*, Fall 2005, in his "From the President" column titled "Good Things Don't Just Happen!" He emphasized the importance of strong Membership, Program, and Nominating Committees at the local level. His appeal was reinforced by Powell's article "Torch Is a Sellable Idea." This theme appeared again in Davis's column "Know Any Teachers?" in *The Torch*, Winter 2005-2006, in which he suggested that teachers would be good candidates for membership. In yet another supportive article in *The Torch* entitled "A Successful Torch Club Needs a 'Spark,'" Powell pointed out that every club needs one or more members who enjoy the Torch concept and through lively discussions generate club-wide curiosity and enthusiasm. In spite of these appeals, by June 2006 membership was 2,350, a further drop of 138 members from 2004. There were seventy clubs. The Washington, DC, Torch Club officially disbanded on July 21, 2005.

Anne Sterling and Ann Dahl, Baltimore Torch Club 75th Anniversary

The proposed budget for 2006-2007 assumed 2,300 regular members at $40 each for $92,000 in revenue. This would lead to an expected shortfall of $9,615! Clearly this was an unsustainable trend. Cost-cutting measures were introduced, such as not printing *The Torchlight* for Fall 2006 and changing the usual in-person Fall Board of Directors Meeting in Norfolk to a telephone conference call. Director Powell presented a report suggesting ways for clubs to find eligible potential members. To further encourage club membership growth and as an incentive the decision was made to issue an annual certificate to the club that had shown the highest percentage of growth. Davis's frustrations with membership trends together with a looming financial crisis found expression in his 2006 "State of Torch" message, in which he acknowledged that people were angry with him, but that "the boat had been sinking for a number of years, that no one had done anything about it and that he hoped someone would."

The 2006 Convention was hosted by the Lehigh Valley Club in Bethlehem, Pennsylvania, June 22-25. The theme was "Heritage and Change." The motto was "Our Goal is to Educate, Entertain and Enrich You." Over 150 members and guests attended. The convention had a surplus of $948.

Alvin Poppen, Wayne Davis display the Chambersburg Charter

The Paxton Award went to Malcom M. Marsden for his article "The Idea of Progress: Battered But Far from Beaten." Gold Torch Awards went to Catherine Fleisher of the Elmira Club and Charles Carlson of the Albany, New York, Club. Fourteen Silver Torch Awards were issued. Lifetime Awards were given to Wilbur Wright of the Genesco, New York, Club and to Harold Rubin of the Albany, New York, Club. The Outstanding Club Award went to the Region 1 Elmira Club.

Attendees were treated to presentations on William Penn, the origins of Crayola and of Martin guitars, and a history of the Lehigh Canal. The tours covered industrial and cultural heritage sites, including visits to areas associated with the local Moravian pioneers. Cultural events included music by the Bach Choir and a performance of Shakespeare's "As You Like It." Dinners were satisfactorily completed with the local delicacies Black Bottom Pie and Moravian Sugar Cake.

July 2006-June 2007

The board of directors consisted of President Anne Sterling, President Elect Stephen T. Toy, Immediate Past President Wayne M. Davis, and Directors Charles E. Carlson (Region 1), John B. Cornish (Region 2), Ann Weller Dahl (Region 3), Edward B. Latimer (Region 4), Linda Porter

(Region 5), George R. Heron (Region 6), John S. Fowler (Region 7), Matthew T. Taylor, Sr. (Region 8), Arthur F. Dawes, III (Region 9), Allan R. Powell (Director-at-Large, Membership), John A. Horner, Jr. (Director-at-Large, Conventions), and Member *ex officio* and Torch Foundation President Ralph C. Falconer. Richard R. Lynch was the board-appointed secretary. Head Office staff included Executive Secretary James V. Strickland, Jr. and Editor R. Patrick Deans.

Ron Bowers, Ann Weller Dahl, and Marino de Medici at Hagerstown's
55th anniversary

The new IATC Board took a more hands-on approach to Torch activities instead of asking for the clubs to provide the momentum. Sterling in her first presidential column offered an ambitious and energetic response to Torch's problems. "Your new IATC board will be investing all possible resources towards spreading the Torch tradition to new towns and cities. We will pursue our outreach in many directions." Additional goals for her biennium term were balancing the budget, growing the Torch Foundation, developing an attractive Torch website, encouraging "intriguing" conventions, and promising more club visits from regional directors and IATC officers. To set an example of serious change, she issued a letter to the entire membership stating that she would accept no reimbursement for travel expenses during her term in office. Other Torch officials followed her example. To address impending financial shortfalls she recommended increasing the member initiation fee to $10, increasing the membership fee by an additional $10, and putting the "Directory of Officers" (aka "The Red Book") online to save printing costs.

Financial statements for the year ending June 30, 2007 indicated a disbursement shortfall of $5,481. In sharp contrast to the financial news, Executive Secretary Strickland reported membership had surged in 2007 by 322 new members to 2,444, for a net gain of ninety-four.

New clubs were established in Shenandoah Valley-Martinsburg, West Virginia, and Blue Ridge-Leesburg, Virginia. There were now seventy-one clubs in the association.

The Richmond, Virginia, Convention was held June 14-17. The theme was "400 Years of American History." Attendance was about 200 members and guests.

The Paxton Award went to Edward P. Blazer for "The Children of Caine and the Genocide Factor." Gold Torch Awards went to John B. Cornish of the Lehigh Valley Club and to H. Jeremy Packard of the Wyoming Valley Club. In addition, nineteen Silver Torch Awards were issued. The Outstanding Club Award went to the Albany Club in Region 1.

In an effort to ease Torch's money troubles, a $10 dues increase to $50 per person annually, effective July 1, 2008, was proposed. A presentation was made to this effect, but the membership was unconvinced and voted to reject the increase.

Entertainment commenced on Thursday with a dinner and a performance of Shakespeare's *The Tempest.* It continued with a tour of the Virginia State Capitol building and a meeting with Governor and Mrs. Kaine. Several reenactors portrayed Thomas Jefferson during different stages of his life and career. Other tours were the famous Shirley Plantation, historic Richmond, the Monticello estate, and the Pumpkin Park National Museum of the Civil War Soldier. A final highlight, to the delight of many delegates, was a special on-stage appearance by the IATC's own band of melodious troubadours.

July 2007-June 2008

The IATC leadership remained the same for Sterling's second year with the exception of three newly elected directors: Theodore E. Haas (Region 3), Richard H. Allen (Region 7), and James J. Owen (Region 8).

Deans had been *The Torch* editor from 1994 until his retirement in 2008. Needing a competent replacement, a delegation from the board approached Past President Taylor and asked him to become the new editor. He readily agreed but with several conditions. He would take the position for five years only. The magazine would be stripped of all opinion columns except for the "From the President" and of all administrative announcements in order to make room for more learned papers. The magazine would be a showpiece of Torch literary talent demonstrating professional quality standards. There was an irksome backlog of approved, engaging articles by Torch members. Taylor began to resolve this issue by printing seven or eight papers in each issue instead of the usual four or five. In the coming years he would include informative guidelines for the proper submission of papers to improve quality and encourage wider member participation. The news and minutiae of the IATC and the clubs would be transferred to *The Torchlight* email newsletter which would be written and edited by Region 1 Director Charles Carlson. In addition, Carlson would maintain and upgrade the IATC's website to provide more immediate interaction with clubs and club members. Taylor served as editor until 2014.

Torch finances were headed for deep deficits. A dues increase was an obvious way to raise additional funds, but the first effort had been soundly defeated at the 2007 Convention. At the urging of Sterling, a second try at raising the annual membership fee was decided upon for the 2008 General Meeting. This effort began with an information packet developed by President Elect Toy in consultation with George Heron and Ted Haas. Toy's fee increase information packet was a masterpiece of reasoned argument and pertinent detail. The fee had not been raised since 1999. The packet fact sheets showed that the cost of living was 25 percent higher and gasoline 78 percent higher. It showed where IATC money was being spent: 30.48 percent on *The Torch*, 13.07 percent on conventions, 12.73 percent on member services and director expenses, and 9.01 percent on management. It showed the efforts that were being made to reduce expenses, such as saving $2,800 on publishing costs by sending out *The Torchlight* electronically at zero cost. The result was that on this second try, the membership voted to increase annual dues from $40 to $50.

Ted Haas, Joanie Powell, Anne Sterling, Allan Powell, George DuBois, Dona Wolfe, and Ann Dahl at the Blue Ridge Leesburg chartering (2007)

The Robert Oldenburg Estate had bequeathed to the Torch Foundation a sizable trust fund to be used for the benefit of the IATC. There was some concern expressed by the board that some Foundation leaders were acting arbitrarily, and were not adhering to the Foundation Bylaws with respect to the handling of Foundation funds.

Clubs had been lost in Houston, Boca Raton, and the Waynesboro area of Pennsylvania. However, a new club had been chartered in High Country, North Carolina. In another hopeful sign, the San Antonio Club had indicated interest in sponsoring a new club in Mexico City. At this point there were sixty-seven active clubs in the IATC.

The 2008 Lancaster, Pennsylvania, Convention was held June 14-17. The theme was "Touch the Past, Celebrate the Future." Attendance was about 180 members and guests. Beginning with a Scottish flavor, the convention's first paper was the provocatively titled "Don't Tell Me What to Do! The Scots-Irish and the Shaping of America." Other thoughtful papers talked about civil rights, presidential elections, and immigration policies.

The 2008 Paxton Award went to Arthur B. Gunlicks, for "Should Turkey Be Admitted to the European Union?" Gold Torch Awards went to Ann Weller Dahl of the Baltimore Club and George DuBois, Jr. of the Frederick, Maryland, Club. Eighteen Silver Torch Awards were issued. The Outstanding Club Award went to the St. Catharines Club in Region 1.

Entertainment included a stirring bagpipe melody and a staging of the musical "Brigadoon." Tours included the National Watch and Clock Museum, a walking tour of historic Lancaster, the Railway Museum of Pennsylvania, and a guided tour of the Amish community.

July 2008-June 2009

The Board of Directors consisted of President Stephen T. Toy, President Elect Edward B. Latimer, Immediate Past President Anne D. Sterling, and Directors Charles E. Carlson (Region 1), John B. Cornish (Region 2), Theodore E. Haas (Region 3), Warner M. Montgomery, Jr. (Region 4), Linda Porter (Region 5), George R. Heron (Region 6), Richard H. Allen (Region 7), James J. Owen (Region 8), Arthur F. Dawes, III (Region 9), Allan R. Powell (Director-at Large, Membership), John A. Horner, Jr. (Director-at-Large, Conventions), and Torch Foundation President Ralph C. Falconer. Headquarters staff consisted of Executive Secretary James V. Strickland, Jr., Administrator Gail Strickland, and Editor A. Reed Taylor. Carlson was made an *ex officio* board member in his capacity as webmaster and *The Torchlight* editor.

President Toy sought to build on the momentum and successes of the Sterling legacy. The revenue from the dues increase that Sterling and Toy had championed gave the IATC a few years of financial stability. In his "From the President" columns he reflected upon the need for the board and Torch members in general to always be open to embracing change. He recounted his positive life-changing experience at the 1991 Buffalo Convention. He praised convention attendance as a way to connect with intriguing people and to renew a sense of personal optimism. "Words in the form of a Torch paper allow us to share knowledge and points of view with clarity. They allow us to open new avenues of thought and to attract those who are intellectually curious."

During the February 2009 Board's conference call, directors received electronic copies of a paper by Matthew Robb from Region 1. This paper outlined a step-by-step plan for appealing to and recruiting younger people to Torch.

A Past Presidents Action Committee chaired by Sterling was formed for the purpose of acting as both an advisory body and as an aid to the board's efforts to generate membership growth. Arthur Goldschmidt, Chair of the History Committee, observed that "for most Torch members it is their club rather than the IATC that encapsulates their experience." This was rather awkward praise for an IATC leadership that was trying to encourage a more national or international perspective. He considered that it would be interesting to study how the admission of women had changed the nature of the Torch experience. Addressing future Torch needs, he recommended that the Torch History Project should be a website.

The organization's financial report for the eleven months ending May 31, 2009 showed an excess of $15,315 from a budget of $123,500. The Lancaster Convention had produced a generous $2,268 surplus for the IATC. This represented a 50 percent split with the host club of the money left over after convention expenses.

Pat & Dave Schooley and Tom Mulkey at a Region 3 Mini Convention

At the 2009 Annual General Meeting, Executive Secretary Strickland reported that as of June 1 there were 2,362 members. Three clubs, in the Waynesboro Area, Pennsylvania, Boca Raton, Florida, and Shenandoah Valley/Martinsburg, West Virginia, had all officially dissolved. The Martinsburg Club had only lasted two years. In May 2008 the High Country Club in Boone, North Carolina, was chartered. High Country was the seventh Torch Club which Allan and Joanie Powell had helped organize. Their next target was a potential club in Annapolis, Maryland. There were now sixty-eight active clubs in twenty-one states and Canada.

The 2009 Fox Valley, Appleton, Wisconsin, Convention was held June 25-28. No theme was offered. Attendance was about 112 members and guests. Papers covered a variety of fields: environmental (park planning), scientific (ethics and stem cell research), and artistic (readings by Ellen Kort, Wisconsin's First Poet Laureate).

The 2009 Paxton Award went to Charles W. Darling for his paper "The Origins of American Involvement in Vietnam." Gold Torch Awards went to John A. Horner, Jr. of the Cleveland, Ohio, Club, and Meredith Rousseau of the Lancaster, Pennsylvania, Club. An impressive twenty-one Silver Awards were issued at this convention. The Outstanding Club Award went to the Buffalo Club in Region 1.

Meanwhile, the fear of financial improprieties, together with the need to make decisions about a $43,800 check from the Oldenburg Estate, caused all five Torch Foundation directors to resign at the Annual General Meeting. A snap election was held during the Appleton Convention. Newly elected were Foundation President Walter J. van Eck, Vice President Ann Weller Dahl, Secretary/Treasurer Dick Lynch, with Board Members Edward Latimer, Stephen Toy, and Thomas Bird.

Entertainment was provided by the North Star Nordic Dancers. Tours included the Paine Art Museum, the Paper Discovery Museum, the famous paperweight collection at the Bergstrom-Mahler Museum, and a visit to the Niagara Escarpment at High Cliff State Park.

July 2009-June 2010

This was the second year of President Toy's term. Fresh faces appearing at the board table were John R.A. Mayer (Director Region 1), Robert G. Bass (Director-at-Large, Conventions) and the newly-elected Foundation President Walter J. van Eck.

Several issues were addressed during this year. A question arose around who had responsibility for preparing club IRS tax returns. It was resolved by requesting that each club prepare its own return. As the result of a different jurisdictional dispute with a local club, the "Convention Manual" was amended to give primacy to IATC Board decisions over local Convention Committees. A "Director's Manual," prepared by George Heron's committee, introduced new directors to the IATC's organizational structure and outlined the directors' responsibilities. Finally, at the 2009 Convention, one delegate purported to represent two clubs simultaneously and requested the subsidies for both clubs! This claim was challenged and the board ruled that members could only be a delegate for one club at a time.

June 2010 membership was reported as 2,268 in sixty-nine clubs. Included in this number was the Westminster, Maryland, Club chartered on June 1, 2010. It had been mentored by Ted and Norine Haas and George DuBois. In a rare failure, Powell had tried unsuccessfully to save the Harrisburg Club.

The 2010 Youngstown, Ohio, Convention was held in June. The theme was "From Rust Belt to Renaissance." Attendance was 130 members and guests. The convention got off to a dramatic start when charismatic Youngstown Mayor Jay Williams presented a paper entitled "Youngstown Renaissance." Other papers talked about the beauty of local parks, the history of labor relations, and even offered a sampling of the songs that inspired the workers' labor movement.

Meredith Rousseau receives the Gold Award from Steve Toy and Ed Latimer (2009)

The Paxton Award went to Barton C. Shaw for "The United States Vice Presidency: Its History and Hard Times." Gold Torch Awards went to Anne Sterling of the Richmond, Virginia, Club, and Leonard W. Weis of the Fox Valley, Wisconsin, Club. At this convention an amazing twenty-four Silver Awards were issued. The Outstanding Club Award 2010 went to the Richmond Club in Region.

The tours covered a planetarium, local church architecture, and museums of American art and of local history.

July 2010-June 2011

The Board of Directors consisted of President Edward B. Latimer, President Elect Charles E. Carlson, Immediate Past President Stephen T. Toy, and Directors John R.A. Mayer (Region 1), John B. Cornish (Region 2), Theodore E. Hass (Region 3), Warner M. Montgomery, Jr. (Region 4), Linda Porter (Region 5), James D. Coppinger (Region 6), Richard H. Allen (Region 7), James J. Owen (Region 8), Arthur F. Dawes, III (Region 9), George R. Heron (Director-at-Large for Membership), Robert G. Bass (Director-at-Large for Conventions), and member *ex officio* and President of The Torch Foundation Walter J. van Eck. Doing double duty was *The Torchlight* Editor and Webmaster Charles E. Carlson. The head office included Executive Secretary Elizabeth Garrett and Editor A. Reed Taylor.

President Latimer brought a wealth of experience and knowledge to the position. One of his "From the President" columns was titled "Changes in My 60 Years with Torch," chronicling his adventures beginning as a member of the Columbia Torch Club in 1950. He observed that "the decline in membership [reflects] demographic shifts in our culture, yet the important things remain the same—close friendships, warm greetings, deep laughs, stimulating papers and conversations—and Torch has been enhanced by technology. I wish you all many blessings and much dancing, long into the future." Torch, he opined, "was founded to foster an inter-professional spirit of good fellowship and mutual intellectual enrichment."

Latimer was of the old school, yet he embraced technology and change. After wishing the Stricklands a happy retirement in June 2010, he welcomed Liz Garrett and Connie Long, of the Newport News firm Association Builders. The Stricklands had been enthusiastic and competent administrators for the IATC, and their rare combination of loyalty and generosity to the organization would be hard to find again. However, technological advances promised a smoother, faster, and more accurate record-keeping system. The Torch head office had been located with the Stricklands in Norfolk, Virginia. Association Builders was based nearby in Newport News, Virginia. The new administrators came with plans for a new website and a state of-the-art data management system. The latter promised improved access to IATC resources such as club dues status and up-to-date membership lists. The board's Fall 2011 meeting was dedicated to creating a strategic plan for membership development. While accepting new technology, President Latimer also encouraged the human touch with tips on how clubs could enhance the experience of prospective members by offering transportation, making guests feel special, providing guests with informative Torch literature, seating guests with "congenial conversationalists," and by personally following up after the meeting. He felt that the board's prime responsibility was extending the Torch legacy into the future by harnessing the advantages of technology while maintaining the values and personal elements that made Torch unique.

President Latimer organized monthly conference calls to improve communication and maintain momentum within the board. At a conference call in September the board adopted the idea of a "records retention policy" which was to be designed by Association Builders. On another issue, membership losses were nearing 10 percent per year. To stem the flow, the board looked at offering "spousal" membership dues discounts. Interestingly, the discussion on this issue turned to the question of how to define a spouse and what were the club's expectations of a member spouse's role and responsibilities. On a happy note, the IATC's resident master policy planner, Leo Kellogg, was nominated for an Honorary Life Membership by his home Albany Club. The motion was passed with enthusiasm and unanimously by the board. At later meetings, the records retention policy was approved, the spousal dues motion was defeated, and a proposal to reduce dues was tabled for future consideration. In May 2011 the Frederick, Maryland, Club offered to host a regional rally.

The Harrisburg, Pennsylvania, and Nashville, Tennessee, Clubs opted to expire in accordance with the proper protocols.

The Hagerstown, Maryland, Convention was held in June 2011. The theme was "A Border State Perspective." Attendance numbers are unavailable. The papers presented covered a broad spectrum of topics including divided loyalties during the Civil War, the influenza epidemic of 1918, the fine arts, and interesting local fossils.

The Paxton Award went to Danny J. Krebs, for "Personal Transportation in the Twenty-first Century and Beyond." Gold Torch Awards went to Linda Porter, Youngstown, Ohio, Club, Theodore Haas, Frederick, Maryland, Club, and Ivan Hrabowsky, St. Catharines, Ontario, Canada, Club. Also issued were fourteen Silver Torch Awards. The Outstanding Club Award 2011 went to the Lehigh Valley Club in Region 2.

Linda Jefferson and Linda Porter (Former Directors of Region 5)

Association Builders presented their first annual report at the convention board meeting. They recommended creating the position of the treasurer or secretary-treasurer. After some discussion, the board decided to have the president elect take on this role. Association Builders reported that in fulfillment of their promise of technological upgrading, the new website was active and that they would be providing training and assistance to the clubs. A special handout on how to use the new capabilities of the website was included in each delegate's convention packet. The new data management system would create club email lists which would be shared both with the club officers and with the relevant regional directors. It was hoped that an interactive website/data management system would ease and clarify record keeping, particularly since a reported 77 percent of clubs did not submit monthly club reports.

To examine the need for revisions and updates, a Bylaw Review Committee was formed consisting of Chair Carlson, Toy, and Sterling. This committee was also tasked with reconsidering the existing IATC logo design. Taylor reminded the board that his term as editor of *The Torch* would end in Spring 2013, so the search for a suitable replacement needed to begin.

Dorothy Driskell, Linda Jefferson (Gold Award), and Dave Hammond, (Columbus Torch Club)

Because the cost of an audit at $5000 to $8000 was beyond existing budget resources, Dick Lynch volunteered to assemble an audit checklist and a group of volunteers to conduct a financial review of the years 2008 to 2010. A special "Financial Review Certificate" was later awarded to Lynch, Robert Murdock, Florence Murdock, and James Schooley upon the successful completion of their task.

At the suggestion of Director-at-Large for Membership George Heron, a strategic planning session dedicated to the membership issue was scheduled for the November 2011 Board meeting. This special session would be led by Heron and Jim Coppinger (Director, Region 6). The recently completed "Directors Manual" was unanimously approved and added to the website resource options with the proviso that only board members would be allowed access.

In further business, Connie Long of Association Builders made a presentation on the IATC Constitution and Bylaws. Each board member received a copy of the constitution, a copy of the current bylaws and a copy of a "Board Fact Sheet." In her presentation Long referred to the lofty goals to which the organization aspired: "The purpose of Torch is to further encourage communications among members, exchange knowledge and create an understanding and develop a breath of thought and culture to foster the highest standards of professional ethics and civic well-being." Every club should have a constitution and bylaws filed with the IATC. Association Builders recommended revisions to the bylaws requiring every club to have at least twenty paid members and to submit a monthly financial report to their regional directors. These last recommendations were administratively desirable goals but not completely anchored in past experience. The IATC Executive Board was to consist of the president, president elect, past president and six-to-twelve additional directors all serving a term of two years. The president could serve a maximum of three consecutive terms. An *ad hoc* committee appointed by the president could "act on matters for the Board, except matters of spending beyond the approved budget." Keeping with the theme of aspirational goals at the Hagerstown Convention, President Latimer formally read into the record a list of Torch values:

> A widely shared conviction in the club that membership in Torch is an honor. Maintenance of high standards of qualification for members. A record of high quality meetings featuring thoughtful and engaging Torch papers. A congenial meeting place where professionals feel comfortable.

Convention tours included the Antietam National Battlefield site, historic downtown Hagerstown, colonial Fort Frederick, and historic homes of Washington County. As a special feature, the convention organizers sponsored a book fair for Torch authors which segued into a public book fair after the convention.

July 2011-June 2012

Five new directors joined President Latimer on the board: Joe Vincent (Region 2), Norine Haas (Region 3), Linda Jefferson (Region 5), Paul Douglas (Region 7), and Felix Almaraz (Region 9).

Charles Darling (Paxton Winner, 2009)

Executive Secretary Garrett prepared a proposed budget for 2012-13 which was reviewed by Charles Carlson and Norine Haas. This budget assumed there would be 2,100 members. It eliminated the $400 stipend for the president of the Foundation and added $1,000 to equalize travel expenses for directors from western regions. Another $1,000 was added to the Membership Fund in anticipation of new clubs in the western states. Some of this new money came from an unanticipated windfall. The cost of producing each issue of *The Torch* dropped from $8,500 to $7,000 after changing the printing vendor. The subscription money paid to Constant Contact to send out *The Torchlight* was questioned and a plan to create an in-house computer server was floated.

Fearing award inflation and devaluation, a decision was made to restrict clubs to one Silver Torch Award for every twenty-five members or portion thereof. Two changes were made to Bylaw VI, Section 2, to address the issues of succession and financial guidance. Change one stated that "if [the] President [is] unable to perform duties then first [the] President Elect and then [the] Past President will take over duties." Change two said that "the President Elect shall chair a Finance Committee that will be responsible for financial reporting and guidance to the Board of Directors. This committee will consist of, at a minimum, the President, President Elect, and a Member at Large."

As with any organization examined over a long period of time with multiple leadership changes and involving many strong personalities, so too did the IATC began to exhibit signs of apathy and discord. Toy, as Chair of the Election Committee, bemoaned the fact that no clubs submitted names for replacement regional directors. Fortunately, the amiable and dedicated incumbent directors all agreed to serve an additional two-year term. The Athens, Georgia, Club, in protest against what it perceived as high fees, unilaterally announced its intention to only pay 50 percent of its dues for 2012-2013. A dispute arose between IATC Executive Secretary Garrett and a board member. Partly this disagreement was about exchanging information concerning convention ribbons and partly it was about club dues. In a telling paragraph from the Portsmouth Convention business session, Garrett in her role as executive secretary recorded that the board member "offered a convention committee report asserting that Liz Garrett had intentionally left it [clubs not paying dues] off the agenda because she is trying to sabotage the convention." Further trouble emerged when President Elect Carlson asserted that the Foundation may have lost its not-for-profit status because of an IRS tax ID number mishandling.

Outside of the above controversies, business continued as normal. Another bylaw change required delegates to attend Business Session I and Business Session II plus the Membership Session at the convention in order to qualify for the IATC reimbursement check.

A report on membership indicated that the numbers were stabilizing with 2,180 in 2010-2011 and 2,179 in 2011-2012! Two more clubs were lost, in Cleveland and Butler County, Ohio, but that loss was partly offset by the formation of a new club in Kearney, Nebraska, in March 2012.

The 2012 Convention was held in Portsmouth/Norfolk, Virginia, during June. Attendance was not recorded. The theme was "400 Years of History, Waterways and Art." The program encompassed talks on human evolution, classical music, calligraphy, and the ironclad USS *Monitor.*

Dick Lynch and Charles Carlson (2012)

The Paxton Award went to Roland F. Moy, "The Thirty Years' Class War: How the Rich Have Won." Gold Torch Awards went to Joseph Vincent of the Lehigh Valley, Pennsylvania, Club, and Edith Reynolds White of the South Hampton Roads, Virginia, Club. In addition, a modest but meaningful nineteen Silver Torch Awards were presented. The Outstanding Club Award went to the Hagerstown, Maryland, Club in Region 3.

The membership session at this convention was particularly comprehensive. Presentations were made on "Membership Initiatives" by George Heron, "An Overview of Statistical Findings and an Overview of Perception Study" by Heron and Coppinger, and a pamphlet template demonstration. The presentations were followed by an idea-sharing discussion to gather audience feedback.

Tours went to the Chrysler Art Museum with its world-class art glass collection, to local displays of stained glass, and to unique local features such as the preserved World War II battleship USS *Wisconsin*.

July 2012-June 2013

The Torch Board of Directors consisted of President Charles E. Carlson, President Elect Norine Haas, Immediate Past President Edward B. Latimer, and Directors John R. A. Mayer (Region 1), Joe Vincent (Region 2), Theodore E. Haas (Region 3), Warner M. Montgomery, Jr. (Region 4), Linda Jefferson (Region 5), James D. Coppinger (Region 6), Paul Douglas (Region 7), James J. Owen (Region 8), Felix Almaraz (Region 9), George R. Heron (Director-at-Large for Membership), Robert G. Bass (Director-at-Large for Conventions), and member e*x officio* and President of The Torch Foundation Anne D. Sterling. The head office was represented by Executive Secretary Elizabeth A. Garrett, *The Torch* Editor A. Reed Taylor, and *The Torchlight* Editor and Webmaster Charles E. Carlson.

74

Torch was fortunate to be able to recruit a world-class organizer as the IATC President— Charles Carlson. He was a past president of the Albany Torch Club, the IATC Webmaster, and the former Region 1 Director. He was a retired civil engineering executive who had held senior consulting positions, a pioneer in computer technology for engineering design and management, and a senior organizer for the Lake Placid Olympic Games. While initially reluctant to take on the arduous duties of IATC President, Carlson made the fortuitous error of sharing the long, dreary drive from Buffalo to Albany with the very persuasive Anne Sterling. Apparently Carlson was not previously aware of how his skills and ambitions meshed so harmoniously with Torch's needs. As president, Carlson's guiding motto was "Building Torch for the Future." With the capable assistance of a new generation of Torch leaders such as President Elect Haas, Region 6 Director Coppinger, and *The Torch* Editor Scott Stanfield, Carlson energized the IATC: "Yes we have challenges, but each challenge creates an opportunity."

In the months that followed, Carlson implemented an action plan. Membership in the IATC and in the clubs was declining about 1 to 2 percent every year. A new membership committee was created under the chairmanship of George Heron. Torch publications were to be revived "to incorporate modern printing, formatting, digital publications and media integration." Director Coppinger offered to update the Torch brochures and to create a new set of promotional literature. To assist in this project and to enliven Torch communications, he hoped to recruit volunteer members with skills in graphics, photography, art, and computer technology. To bankroll the action plan, Haas would chair a new Finance and Budget Committee with a special emphasis on addressing plans for the future, such as designating funds for club growth. Funds for membership and club development had already been approved at the Portsmouth Convention Annual General Meeting. Director Jerry Bass, Member-at-Large for Conventions, would encourage the expansion of regional mini-meetings to enhance inter-club contact and mutual support. Past President Latimer would chair the Nomination Committee. His job would be to seek out energetic new leaders to join the board.

Spring 2013 was the last edition of *The Torch* edited by Taylor. With the advice and assistance of Taylor, a new communication/editorial team was formed. President Elect Haas noted that "I'm excited about the changes that are planned for the Torch magazine. Perhaps I am even more excited that it is a team effort of membership and our new editor."

In her Executive Secretary's Report for 2013, Garrett reported that Association Builders' hosting service (a subcontractor) had been sold and that this would temporarily disrupt service to the IATC. Furthermore, an increased workload from tax filings for larger corporations meant that Association Builders no longer found small accounts such the IATC to be cost-efficient, and therefore had decided to raise its fee from $28,600 to $33,904. Bylaw amendments created two new "youth" categories of membership. The "Young Professional" membership was for students thirty-five years and older. It offered membership at 50 percent of regular cost. The second category was "Professional-in-Training" targeted at younger students who would pay the regular fee but would need to be sponsored by the college that they attended. There were already student members in the Lincoln and Hastings, Nebraska, Clubs.

In his role as *The Torchlight* editor, Carlson described the successful efforts of Ted and Norine Haas to mentor smaller clubs in Region 3, which resulted in membership growth. Further good news was the creation, as a result of the efforts of the Lincoln Torch Club, of two new clubs in Kearney and Hastings, Nebraska. The new clubs added sixty new members in 2012. A third new club, Southeast, Nebraska, was formed in May 2013. Sadly, the Firelands/Sandusky, Ohio, Club closed in October 2012.

The 2013 Torch Convention was held in Columbia, South Carolina, in June. Attendance was seventy-five members and guests. The theme was "Famously Hot—Historically Cool." The papers were diverse and intriguing. They varied from the development of thinking machines to ancient empires to a legal view of antebellum South Carolina to the benefits of saving your Confederate money.

The Paxton Award went to Leland W. Robinson, for "The Self: Perspectives from East and West." No Gold Torch Awards were given this year. However, thirteen Silver Torch Awards were given to club members. Honorary Lifetime Memberships were awarded to Charles Greeb, Jr. and Reed Taylor. The winner of the Outstanding Club Award 2013 was not recorded.

The tours covered historic plantations, Civil War battle sites and historic sections of Columbia, plus the option of taking either a lake cruise or a train adventure!

July 2013-June 2014

This was Carlson's second and last year as IATC President. The board welcomed five fresh faces around the table. The new directors were: returning veteran Richard Lynch (Region 1), Meredith Rousseau (Region 2), Michael H. Parsons (Region 3), and George Conklin (Region 8). The directorship of Region 9 was vacant. The new executive secretary was Jennifer Morrone from Association Builders.

The new editor, Scott Stanfield, started work with the Fall 2013 issue of *The Torch*. The Communications Committee chaired by Coppinger, together with Stanfield and Region 8 Director Conklin, decided on a new look for the magazine. The dimensions were reduced and it was printed on magazine stock which resulted in a considerable financial savings. These savings were then used to introduce new features such as a four-color, four-sided cover, new fonts, and an increased use of graphics. The response to the new look was encouraging. One reader, J.C. Owens of the Boulder Club, wrote: "The fall edition is one of the best issues I have ever seen, really excellent articles, a very good selection of topics, and very well written." Conklin, who had previously edited an online academic journal, sought to make articles in *The Torch* increasingly searchable and easily electronically available. Also, consideration was given to creating a response blog to engage and report the readers' reactions to the magazine articles. Similarly, there were thoughts of creating a review blog for members' books and publications. Conklin established an online version of the magazine available at www.thetorchmagazine.org. Both the print and online editions of *The Torch* were compatible with both academic and publications standards.

In his "From the President" column entitled "Planning the Future of Torch," Carlson mentioned that the future would be the theme of the Board's Winter Retreat and "Blue Sky" ideas session. This session was to be led by President Elect Haas and it would be the first step in a Torch-wide strategic plan. Topics to be discussed would be a look at the present and future demographics of Torch, member and local club support, the IATC website, IATC communications and publications, possible new and enhanced member services (a new online Torch apparel store was already active), local clubs and membership developments, development of a clearer view of a viable Torch, and what it would take to meet the challenges of tomorrow. Communication and participation would be improved through an early website posting of the draft 2014 -2015 budget and other general meeting items that needed membership approval. It was expected that local clubs would thus have time to meet and discuss how the club would vote.

Membership had been sliding at about 2 percent per year. The membership turnover rate was about 10 percent, but new club recruits had stabilized membership at 2,200 with even the possibility of a slight increase. The Knoxville Club had disbanded and the Chicago Club's continued existence was questionable. Still, seventeen clubs had a membership increase of over 10 percent and another thirty of the current sixty-seven clubs had some growth. The efforts of President Elect Francis Moul had resulted in three new Nebraska clubs being added to the roster. The grant program had been moderately successful. Budget money had been made available to local clubs for membership, recruitment, and development. Foundation money supplemented these funds and was available for recruitment and retention or printing of promotional literature. Moul had collected voluntary donations totaling $3,000 from the Saginaw Valley, Michigan, and Lincoln, Nebraska, Clubs to be spent on fresh initiatives for developing new clubs.

The 2013 Convention had proposed a new bylaw called the "household membership initiative" which needed approval at the 2014 Annual General Meeting. This bylaw change would reduce the dues of the second member of a household by 50 percent. It was expected to reduce current revenues by 5 percent, but would recoup money by encouraging spouses and other family members to become full members instead of just frequent guests. Because of the aging membership, a new "Young Member Initiative" was being proposed.

Communication was important to a Torch revitalization. *The Torch* was of key importance because it was the only item produced by the IATC that reached 100 percent of the membership. The Communications Committee was planning new and expanded features, partly to address new reading media such as Kindle and iPad. Conklin had formatted a digital edition of *The Torch* and had arranged to index the magazine on the EBSCO data base. *The Torchlight* newsletter's goal was six email issues at the rate of one every two months. Constant Contact, the email contact service, already had 2,135 member email addresses on file. The current open rate was 40 percent of messages sent out, but there were hopes of improving upon that. The previous website host had been sold, so it was decided to find a new host and revamp the IATC website with the help of Mark Dahmke of Infoanalytics in Lincoln, Nebraska.

The IATC could no longer afford the services of Association Builders. The decision was made to move to Jim Coppinger's company Quadrant II Marketing, LLC. Coppinger would resign as a director and be hired as IATC's new executive secretary. Finally, there was good news from the Finance Committee of Haas, Carlson, and Toy. The IATC was financially solvent! By changing the administrator, finding cheaper publication costs, and with service and website changes, the committee had transformed a deficit of $8,000-$12,000 into a surplus of $6,000! This optimistic projection was somewhat misleading since the draft budget showed total income $107,985, total expenses $102,402 for a net surplus of $5,583. In fact the total income was $102,660, total expenses were $102,090, and the net excess was $570, a considerably smaller surplus but still a surplus.

The 2014 Torch Convention was held in St. Catharines, Ontario, Canada, in June. Attendance was about 109 members and guests. The theme was "200 Years of Peace between Friends/Deux Cents Ans de Paix Entre Amis." The eclectic presentations included "The 1812 Legacy: A First Nations Perspective" presented by a local Iroquois historian, "China's Political System and the Future of Democracy" given by a leading Canadian China expert, and "Canada's Health Care System" delivered by a local physician.

The 2014 Paxton Award went to Henry Ticknor, for "Whose Life Is It, Anyway?" Gold Torch Awards went to Linda D. Jefferson, of the Columbus, Ohio, Club, and Francis D. Moul of the Lincoln, Nebraska, Club. Twelve Silver Torch Awards were issued to deserving club members. The Outstanding Club Award was not recorded.

The convention attendees were treated to singing, dancing, and hilarity at the Oh Canada, Eh? dinner theatre. Tours visited War of 1812 battle sites, followed the route of the Welland Canal, and viewed the sights of Niagara Falls in Canada.

The decade's definitive statement on Torch International's hopes and dreams was given by Carlson in his farewell "The State of Torch" speech at the St. Catharines Convention. He observed that in 2013-2014 the IATC was in transition. Everything was in a state of change and movement—a new website was planned, there was a new executive secretary, a new editor of *The Torch*, an increasingly affordable and member-friendly magazine, and a great many additional initiatives had been introduced or were planned. It had been a good year. Carlson was optimistic.

Chapter 5: July 2014–June 2024

Written by Douglas Punger
Researched by Chris Atzberger

Overview of the Decade

At last, we reach the final decade of Torch, a decade of major challenges, controversies and surprising sustainability. The COVID-19 pandemic, which began in January 2020 and lasted more than two years, challenged Torch and many other organizations, institutions, and businesses to survive, but survive it did. In response to federal, state, and local lockdown rules most clubs were unable to meet in person for many months and for some clubs, more than a year. The pandemic forced the cancellation of two annual conventions, the first time successive conventions had been canceled since World War II. Those clubs with the technological ability to offer meetings via the Zoom online meeting site created a new way of engagement and opened up a door to communication that would forever change Torch. Unquestionably, zooming saved Torch and helped it survive this calamity.

Torch also survived some major controversies. One of its longer-serving presidents was censured and barred from holding any current or future office with the IATC for a period of five years. However, the bar on service was lifted within a year. A second board member was censured and barred from all IATC offices and from attendance at IATC events. The seeds of the controversy began in the Spring of 2017 with the first contested election for the vice presidency in the history of Torch. A vigorous campaign led by one candidate's supporters sparked flames of discord that were never quite extinguished. The same member ignited another controversy over an article published in *The Torch* in Fall 2020. But his most provocative act, based on an internal investigation, was intentionally misappropriating the Torch logo. These overlapping and interconnected controversies consumed the leadership of Torch for a significant period of time and may still linger in the background.

Despite these challenges and controversies, Torch survived. When this decade began there were about 2,190 members and between sixty-seven and seventy active clubs. In the spring of 2022, as the country and Torch were reopening after months of lockdowns due to the pandemic, there were 1,527 members in fifty-one active clubs. Since then, the board has approved an innovative strategic plan and provided a toolkit for local club leaders to recruit new members. Several board members are actively engaged in incubating new clubs. While we will not achieve the goals set many years ago to have 5,000 members in one hundred clubs by the end of our first century, still Torch has powered through the obstacles and continues to vigorously rebuild.

July 2014-June 2015

The single word that described the 2014-2015 Torch year would be "transition" as Charles Carlson, outgoing IATC President, wrote in "The State of Torch," a paper published in *The Torch* in Fall 2014.

The IATC Board terminated its contract with Association Builders (AB) in June 2014 due to its increasing costs and declining revenue from membership dues. AB had served the IATC well since 2010. Jim Coppinger, of the Kalamazoo, Michigan, Club, a Regional Director and a principal in the marketing firm Quadrant Marketing LLC (QM), was hired as Executive Secretary effective July 1. He had submitted a comprehensive plan to reduce costs and increase the level of service to Torch members with fees about 25 percent less than AB.

James Coppinger

Leadership included President Norine Haas, Immediate Past President Charles E. Carlson, President Elect Francis Moul, Executive Secretary James D. Coppinger, President Emeritus Edward B. Latimer, Head of Finance Committee Francis Moul, Directors Richard Lynch (Region 1), Meredith Rousseau (Region 2), Anne Thomas (Region 3), Flynn Warren (Region 4), Linda Jefferson (Region 5), Richard Fink (Region 6), Francis Moul, acting (Region 7), George Conklin (Region 8), Roger Kramer (Region 9), George R. Heron (Director-at-Large, Membership), Robert G. Bass (Director-at-Large, Conventions), Richard Lynch (member *ex officio*,

Torch Foundation President), and Scott Stanfield (Editor of *The Torch*). It is notable that four of these leaders were women, evidencing that the IATC had accepted women as members and leaders after decades of excluding them from membership.

Norine Haas was a longtime leader of the Frederick, Maryland, and Westminster, Maryland, Clubs. She graduated from the Temple University School of Nursing. She retired after many years as CEO of the Frederick County Mental Health Association.

Both Haas and Coppinger supported many technological improvements in the administration of Torch. Beginning in the fall of 2014, Torch papers had to be submitted via email from the author's club secretary or treasurer to verify that the author was a club member and had presented the paper at that club. Coppinger planned to use web-based technology to update and maintain membership rosters online.

The IATC amended its bylaws at the June 2014 Convention to create the Family Membership category. Apparently, there were some questions about who might benefit from this. As Haas explained in the September 2014 issue of *The Torchlight,* after a first family member paid the regular dues of $50, a second family member such as a spouse, parent, son, daughter, or sibling, would be eligible for membership at $25, half the regular rate.

Haas appointed a secretary and a treasurer from members of the board. Lynch agreed to serve as treasurer and Rousseau as secretary.

Among the major accomplishments of the new IATC leadership was the development and approval of a comprehensive business plan at the 2015 Winter Conference in Baltimore. The business plan was to be a financial and organizational foundation for the next decade, to the Torch Centennial in 2024 and beyond. It included priorities, funding objectives, sources of potential growth, and deadlines for goals and milestones. Action steps were identified, including: professional to professional, a method for club development; membership training for regional directors and local club officers; information kits for prospective members; publicity efforts utilizing all available media, especially the website and social media; using *The Torch* to tell the Torch story; adding college student members; recruiting young professional members. The plan established a Finance Committee and defined who was authorized to sign a check based on the amount of the check. It required a yearly budget process. It also set aside reserve funds for conferences, membership development, the History Project, and the Century Fund.

Coppinger and Haas presented the idea of publishing a book to celebrate the IATC's Centennial in 2024. Thus, the seed was planted in February 2015 for the book you are reading.

A Torch Travel Program was reported at the April 2015 Board Meeting. The first trip was scheduled to Cuba in 2016.

Conklin, Haas, and Lynch drafted a policy concerning accommodating individuals with impairments at all IATC functions, especially the annual convention. The board approved that policy on June 9, 2015.

The Century Fund was instituted to facilitate the 2024 celebration of the First Century of Torch's existence and enable it to reach the goal set in 2014 of one hundred clubs and 5,000 members by the year of the centennial. It would provide extra funding to hold receptions and purchase promotional materials and publicity that would assist in ensuring a celebration worthy of the effort to be made over the next decade to reach these goals.

In January 2015 *The Torchlight* reported that Torch had ninety new members. Roanoke Valley was recognized for adding eight members. A push to renew the Portland, Maine, Club was highlighted. The June membership report for 2015 recorded 2,270 active members in sixty-three clubs. Of that number, there were 2,093 regular members, 142 Household members, fourteen At-Large members, two Student members, and two Young Professional members. At the convention Moul reported that the Erie, Roanoke, Leesburg, and Chambersburg Clubs had all experienced new member growth and a new club was chartered in Fredericksburg, Virginia. However, the Baltimore, Knoxville, and Ashville Clubs were dissolved.

Ted and Norine Haas (Columbus, 2016)

The 2015 Convention was held in Lincoln, Nebraska, the home club of Thomas Carroll. Its theme was "Great Plains, Great Ideas." Among the interesting papers delivered were: "Will Nuclear Weapons Ever Be Used? A New Triad Emerges from the Historic Nuclear Triad," and "German Prisoners of War in Nebraska: An Unforeseen Opportunity."

The Paxton Award was given to Roger A. Hughes of the Des Moines Torch Club for his paper "The Singularity: Technology and the Future of Humanism." He asked what will happen when machines evolve to the point they are just as intelligent as humans? More importantly, what will happen when machines become more intelligent? Does Humanism have a future? (Was the author predicting the coming of Artificial Intelligence?)

After a year of development, the Century Project was communicated to all Torch leaders at the convention.

Stanfield and Coppinger discussed the introduction of more color pages and additional features to *The Torch*. They also streamlined, through e-communication, document submission and review. Through the efforts of Conklin a newly formatted digital edition of *The Torch* was made available online, making it available to almost every library in the world through online search. Mark Dahmke, CEO of Infoanalytics of Lincoln, Nebraska, agreed to redesign and host the website. Coppinger shared a plan to scan Torch papers from the past stored in the Ohio State University Archives and to make them available electronically with software to make those documents keyword searchable.

The following bylaw amendments were approved at the 2015 Convention:
- The "Family Membership" category was changed to "Household Membership."
- Another new category of membership was added: "Honorary Lifetime Membership" which could be bestowed upon any person.
- The "president elect" position was changed to "vice president."
- The officers clause was amended to add a treasurer and a secretary.
- The dues clause was amended to require one annual payment by February 1 rather than two semi-annual payments.

July 2015-June 2016

This year the board and officers were the same as in 2014-2015, with the exception of Director Anne H. Thomas (Region 3) and Director Martha Gadberry (Region 7). Apparently Vice President Francis Moul became ill sometime before the December 8, 2015 board meeting. Director Dick Fink of Region 6 was recorded in the minutes as interim vice president and chair of the Finance Committee.

Robert Kuzelka, Lincoln Torch Club, and Reed Taylor (Columbus 2016)

In August 2015 Coppinger stated that the 2014-2015 fiscal year ended with a deficit of $12,705.44. Two major contributing factors were delegate reimbursement checks at $250 each for two conventions (2014 and 2015) which doubled the costs, and travel reimbursement for board members to attend the 2015 Convention in Lincoln which averaged $1,000, considerably higher than in the past.

A decision to split Region 1 into two regions was made at the October 13 Board Meeting due to both the number of clubs and the enormous geographical territory in the region. The clubs in western New York and Erie, Pennsylvania, plus St. Catharines in Ontario, would form Region 10, led by Regional Director Tim Spaeder, president of the Erie Club. Region 1 Director Diana Hinchcliff, past president of the Albany Club, was placed in charge of the clubs in eastern New York, Maine, and Massachusetts.

At the February meeting in Baltimore, the centennial goal of reaching one hundred clubs and 5,000 members by 2024 was reconfirmed by all. Several characteristics in selecting sites for new clubs were discussed, including: communities that were not too large or too small; sites within a fifty-mile radius of an existing club; communities with a college or university; communities with a concentration of like-minded Torch people; and communities with one individual who was a "sparkplug" — a self-directed individual with drive, energy, and enthusiasm for such an undertaking. Each regional director was asked to identify at least one community in their region for a potential new club.

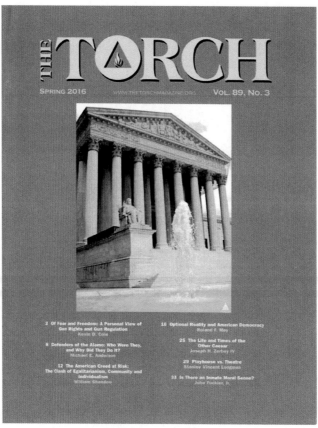

The Torch, Spring 2016

CENTURY PROJECT

Calling all Torch Clubs

We need your participation! The goal to be reached by 2024–**one hundred Torch Clubs** and **5,000 members** by Torch International's ***100th birthday***! To celebrate we plan to have the centennial convention in Minneapolis where it all started. And we plan to have a great time!

What are we doing to reach the goal?

New clubs have been added in the past three years and plans are in the works for several more. There is a continuing emphasis on growth in currently existing clubs, along with urging clubs to reach out and found other new clubs. Four clubs have had double digit membership growth this year, one with the equivalent of a new club by itself.

College students and young professionals are being recruited to clubs to bring needed age diversity and new voices to Torch.

How are we promoting club growth and local club buy in for this major goal?

The Torch magazine has been remade into an attractive, colorful publication that is now online in thousands of libraries. Torch members will be visiting Cuba next year on a ***Torch Tour***—a new wrinkle! The Torch website is being improved and a new data base is being constructed to make it much easier for local Torch clubs to interface with the Torch international office. We're in Wikipedia and have a Torch blog. Torch is on the move!

Are there financial implications in implementing The Century Project?

Yes, based on recent experience, this major effort could cost about $6,000 a year for the next nine years. Fortunately, the ***Torch Foundation*** has initiated new club startup funds to help finance this work, with individuals and clubs involved. Your club is invited to contribute, or individuals can make tax deductible gifts via the Foundation to the new club startup fund.

Clubs and individuals are also encouraged to send contributions to the Torch Foundation's ***New Club Development Fund*** in memory of long-time members who have died. For instructions to send contributions, see www.torch.org.

Membership development funding from the IATC is available for use by clubs. Each Torch club needs to grow. At minimum, considering attrition, a 10% growth rate per year is needed just to stay even. A desirable club membership goal is at least 30 to 50 members or more, in order to have a good diversity of paper presentations. An excellent paper is still the key to a successful Torch meeting.

What do we need to do to make this work?

The key to success will depend upon leadership from the Regional Directors, as well as cooperation from local clubs to relay this information to every member of our Association. Clubs also need to be prepared for prospective guests with information kits that include the ***Torch Is...***sheet, a copy of ***The Torch*** magazine, local club information, and a membership application form.

What about new club formation?

It is essential that Regional Directors work with clubs to identify communities that are likely prospects for new club starts, and a list of sparkplug members of the local club and the new communities who can help start a club. Contact your Regional Director to see about available resources for travel, supplies and luncheon or dinner expenses for potential members. A major consideration when planning a new club start: The key is to find community leaders who can invite 20-30 friends to the event. Ask if IATC officers are available to attend.

Begin now! Plan activities such as luncheon or dinner receptions to start new clubs or special guest nights to introduce prospective members to Torch. Prepare information kits to distribute to guests and prospective members. Invite professional men and women who may be potential members to dinner as your guest. Plan a special guest night, with an enhanced presentation, menu and information about Torch. Ask guests to sign up as members on the spot, paying the initiation fee and receiving new member kits. Order the kits ahead of time, in any quantity.

If your club holds a special luncheon or evening event to introduce prospective members to Torch, the IATC will reimburse your club for the lunch or dinner of every person who fills out an application and provides a check for the application fee.

Seek out introductions to college presidents or deans of students at local universities for permission to subsidize one or two college students as Torch members of existing or new clubs. Check out young professional groups or leadership training classes that many cities sponsor. All are ready reservoirs of potential young Torch members.

There is an old saying that there is no burden if everyone lifts. To bring a lot of new life to our beloved Torch organization, we all need to lift.

Francis Moul, IATC Vice President and Membership Chair. Questions? Contact by email: fmoul1@neb.rr.com or call Francis at **402-423-0949**

Francis and Maxine Moul, Lincoln Torch Club (Columbus Convention 2016)

The board discussed the structure of the annual convention. Three areas of focus were identified: business, social, and educational. It was expressed that the social aspect should be a priority and that less time should be spent on conducting business. The consensus was that the convention should be to "serve our local clubs, members, and officers" and to put a human face on the IATC.

Lynch moved that the board adopt the policy that all dues for clubs outside the United States be paid in US dollars, which was unanimously approved. However, in April the St. Catharines Club sent a check in US dollars as agreed but reduced the actual dues payment to adjust St. Catharines dues to Canadian value, which was not the agreement. The board asked the Finance Committee to resolve this issue.

The Torchlight for March highlighted the Torch tour to Cuba. The feedback from members who went was very positive. They enjoyed the educational and cultural aspects of the adventure led by an excellent Road Scholar guide. Since the first Torch Travel adventure was a success, a second trip was selected, to Costa Rica and the Panama Canal, for March 2017.

In March the "Redbook" returned in an electronic form on the IATC website. It contained a listing of clubs and a directory of officers and their contact information. Torch was given a new tagline: "Torch: A Forum for Reasoned Discourse."

Haas announced that she had established a Centennial Committee to lead the association's planning for the celebration in 2024. The committee members were Charles Carlson, Stephen

Toy, Ann Weller Dahl, Ed Latimer, Janet Moy LaMonica, Connie Turner, Mark Dahmke, Anne Sterling, and Tim Spaeder.

Haas's "President's Column," in *The Torch* Spring 2016, urged clubs to create a website if they didn't already have one, and to consider using social media to promote club programs.

As of June 1, there were sixty-three active clubs with a total membership of 2,401. Lynch reported that the Grand Rapids Torch Club had dissolved, as did the Portland, Western Maine, Club. However, two new clubs were established–one in Fredericksburg, Virginia, and one in Wayne, Nebraska.

The theme of the 2016 Convention in Columbus, Ohio, was "Come Discover Columbus...." The program began with "A Conversation with President Edward Orton: First President of The Ohio State University" presented by Ronald St. Pierre, Professor Emeritus. It was followed by "Public Health: Stories from the Field" presented by Susan A. Tilgner, Franklin County Commissioner of Public Health. The final presentation was "Ohio and Presidential Elections" given by Herbert B. Asher, Professor Emeritus of Political Science.

The Paxton Award winner was John P. Lewis for his paper "Forbidden Words." His paper made three points about these immodest words. First, words are powerful. The old expression "sticks and stones can break my bones but words can never hurt me" simply is not true. Second, words and their meanings continually change. English is a living language. Third, taboo language can do many different things. Cursing can be offensive or it can be funny. It can incite animosity or it can cement friendships. It all depends on context.

Dick Lynch and John P. Lewis (2016 Paxton winner, Columbus Convention)

At the business meeting it was reported that the IATC was in good financial standing with a surplus of $23,131. There were 2,240 members last year and 2,427 this year, an increase of 187. Coppinger reported a number of instances where clubs had people on their rosters who were no longer members, meaning that last year's number might be inflated and our growth actually much higher. Moul proposed hiring a part-time professional consultant, board member Diana Hinchcliff, to work specifically on new club development. He pledged $500 per month for one year to assist in covering the cost if there were matching contributions. Flynn Warren, Charles Carlson, and Tim Spaeder also pledged amounts to the effort.

The bylaws were amended to read "The annual IATC dues for Torch Clubs outside the United States shall be paid in U.S. dollars." The previous provision allowed dues for Torch Clubs outside the US to be paid in US dollars equal to one-half the difference between US dollars and the local currency. The St. Catharines Club approved this change.

Tours included the new Arthur G. James Cancer Hospital, the Richard M. Ross Heart Hospital, the Ohio Statehouse, the Billy Ireland Cartoon Library and Museum, the Historic Ohio Theater, the Ohio State University campus, and the James Thurber Home.

You never know who will show up at a convention.

July 2016-June 2017

New leadership included President Dick Fink, Vice President David Hammond, Past President Norine Haas, Co-Directors Dorothy Driskell and Linda Porter (Region 5), and Director Mark Dahmke (Region 7). President Elect Francis Moul declined the office of president due to ill health, but continued to serve on the board in his role on membership and new club development.

In August Diana Hinchcliff and Mark Dahmke were hired for a six-month pilot project to assist struggling Torch clubs in Region 1 and Region 6. Fink reported at the Winter Board Meeting on the efforts of Hinchliff, Dahmke, Moul, and others to identify and support struggling clubs and identify locations for new clubs. Hinchcliff led a discussion on assessing the strengths of Torch Clubs and key indicators for identifying struggling clubs. Fink noted that as of January 1, IATC had sixty-three clubs and 2,116 members from a high of 105 clubs and 5,300-plus members in the 1970s. He proposed hiring a full-time executive director and a part-time paid information technology person to help clubs manage their data and share it with the IATC database. The board approved a 10 percent dues increase to cover the additional cost of paid staff, to be voted on at the 2017 Convention.

In January, just prior to the Winter meeting, both Vice President Hammond and Past President Haas resigned, she due to health reasons, he for reasons unknown. This was a surprise to the IATC Board and created an issue of leadership and succession not previously experienced. Chair of the Nomination Committee Moul emailed all Torch members, seeking nominations for interim vice president, and only received a self-nomination from George Conklin with documentation from two clubs supporting him. The board elected him interim vice president at the Winter meeting.

A Torch member raised questions about the procedure for election of the vice president at the upcoming 2017 Convention, making reference to the Torch Bylaws and the "Election Manual." On February 20 a group of former IATC presidents met by conference call, reviewed the timing of Hammond's resignation, and recommended to the board: (1) that the president appoint a new Nomination Committee chaired by a past president as required by the bylaws; (2) that President Fink make clear his intentions regarding the second year of his two-year term; (3) that a schedule for the election be established; and (4) that the "Election Manual" and "Torch Bylaws" be posted on the Torch website. They also recommended that Charles Carlson assume the position of immediate past president due to Haas's resignation, which he accepted.

The second Torch Tour, to Costa Rica and Panama, occurred in March.

Stephen Toy, a former president, agreed to serve as chair of the Nomination Committee. Two Torch members ran for the position of vice president: Conklin, who was elected interim vice president at the Winter Meeting, and Hinchcliff, who was leading the effort to increase membership and clubs. Both were very qualified candidates. However, this election was significantly different from any previous one. There had never been a contested election before. In addition, there was some "campaigning" by email in support of one of the candidates. This was also unusual and not favorably received by some members.

In April Toy gave an overview of the significant events that led to a dispute over the standing of Hinchcliff's nomination for vice president. In response the board approved the following resolution: "The Board of Directors of the IATC hereby ratifies and confirms the actions and decisions of the Nominating Committee relating to the timeframes and procedures for the election of candidates for the Office of Vice President." Prior to the convention, Toy informed Torch Club leaders of the procedures for the election of officers at the convention, noting that there were two candidates for vice president. He told the members they could vote by email, US mail, or in person as delegates to the convention.

Hammond, co-chair of the Columbus 2016 Convention Committee, shared the convention evaluations. Factoring out Columbus Club members and IATC Board members, about forty people attended the convention. The number one reason for not attending was cost. The registration fee, travel, and lodging totaled about $1,000. Three proposals were brought before the board concerning conventions: (1) to raise the club delegate reimbursement rate from $250 to $300; (2) to ask clubs to send delegates and underwrite all or part of their costs; and (3) to ask the IATC, rather than the host club, to pay for hotel conference room rentals, meals etc., to avoid sales tax. As a 501(c)(4), some states might grant the IATC a sales tax exemption, saving more than $1,000. In October the board approved increasing the club reimbursement from $250 to $300.

It was announced that the 2018 Torch Convention could not be held in Erie. Roger Kramer said the San Antonio Torch Club would be willing to host it and the board approved.

Also at the April Board Meeting Coppinger reported that approximately $98,000 in dues would be collected for the 2017-2018 year based on a budget of $111,000, suggesting a shortfall of $11,000 to $12,000. Several board members pledged not to seek reimbursement for regional travel expenses. Others volunteered not to seek reimbursement for their convention expenses. Due to the budget shortfall, the board agreed to recommend a dues increase at the 2017 Annual Convention for final approval.

Due to an increase in the workload at his marketing firm Executive Secretary Coppinger submitted his resignation in April 2017. Fink appointed Interim Vice President Conklin to chair the search committee for a new executive secretary. Anne Sterling volunteered to serve on the search committee.

As of June there were sixty-three active clubs with a total membership of 2,272, with 2,017 regular members, 217 Household members, twelve Honorary members, six Student members, and seven Young Professional members.

The 2017 Convention was held in Kalamazoo, Michigan. The theme was "Ahead of the Curve: Vision Drives Community." Very enjoyable events were held Thursday night, including "Pass the Torch," a mentor night to introduce students and young professionals to Torch, followed by an "After Glow Party" at the Park Club. Among the presentations were "The Kalamazoo Promise: How Every Kalamazoo Public High School Graduate Can go to College for Free" by Von Washington, Executive Director of Community Relations Kalamazoo Promise, and "What Does a Conductor Do?" by Barry Ross, Professor Emeritus of Music, Kalamazoo College, former Assistant Conductor of the Kalamazoo Symphony Orchestra.

The Paxton Award winning paper was "Race Matters" by Steve Sterrett. According to the author, we cannot significantly improve the relationship between police and many African Americans until we end the War on Drugs and mass incarceration. We also must change our expectations of the police. We, as a society, have placed police officers on the front line of a War on Drugs that in reality has been an assault on poor, largely African American communities. Police officers bore the brunt of the battle, although behind the scenes and providing tactical support and encouragement was the whole prison-industrial complex of courts and penitentiaries.

At the convention business meeting Coppinger stated that all but one club was current on the year's dues and yet the association was $11,599 below budgeted dues income. He also said it was possible that the convention would be in deficit and funds might need to be drawn from the convention "rainy day" savings account.

Conklin, interim IATC vice president and chair of the finance committee, announced that the IATC board, at its June 15 business meeting, voted to rescind a recommendation for a dues increase for 2017-2018. He acknowledged that the board believed that the negative atmosphere surrounding this year's election of officers created a climate that would not be receptive to any increase in dues.

At the convention Coppinger administered the counting of the votes for vice president. Conklin was declared the incoming IATC Vice President.

The board discussed adding a provision to the bylaws about removing a member from the board in the event of misconduct, illness, malfeasance, or other related issues. An *ad hoc* committee was formed to draft proposed bylaws amendments.

July 2017-June 2018

IATC President Dick Fink resigned on August 31. Vice President Conklin became interim president. Fink gave no explanation for his resignation.

At the August 8 Board Meeting the search committee for a new executive secretary recommended contracting with Organization Management Group, Inc. (OMG), a Virginia-based company. The initial cost for their services was $49,000 per year, which was $9,000 less than budgeted. OMG and the IATC Board reached a scope-of-work agreement including: a process for the selection of the executive secretary from OMG's staff, coordinating meetings and conference calls, managing financial reports, maintaining the membership database, producing membership reports and new member packets, coordinating office workflow, responding to member requests, assisting with annual conventions, hosting the website, and assisting in producing publications including *The Torch*. OMG was to begin September 1. In a winter 2018 message to Torch, Conklin introduced OMG.

The financial statement showed IATC had received $90,530 in dues, about $10,000 less than budgeted. OMG reported that a few clubs had not paid their dues. The Boulder, Colorado, Club was withdrawing from Torch. IATC membership had declined to about 1,800 members.

The 2018 Convention was held in San Antonio, Texas, in the historic Menger Hotel, which opened in 1859. The theme was "Carry the Torch to San Antonio." On the first day a presentation was made on the history and culture of San Antonio.

The 2018 Paxton Award winner was "American Political Economy: Forty Years of Metastatic Normality" by Roland Moy. According to Moy, economic growth in the United States had slowed since the 1970s, perhaps a return to historic trends. But inequality had rapidly increased. A new normal which reversed the trend might eventually happen.

At the June 21 Board Business Meeting, the OMG executive secretary reported on the progress of Facebook advertisements. However, Jim McNeely said he did not receive any calls from potential members as a result of the Facebook ad.

The Witte Museum was the site of the formal dinner on Saturday night.

July 2018-June 2019

As a result of many resignations, a number of new people were elected to the IATC Board in 2018. President George Conklin was elected for a two-year term. It appears that Gerald Stulc was nominated and elected vice president at the convention but resigned shortly thereafter. Dorothy Driskell from the Columbus, Ohio, Club was appointed by the board as interim vice president. Directors were: Gerald Stulc (Region 1), Jim McNeeley (Region 2), Lynn Bernard (Region 3), Doug Johnson (Region 6), and Walter van Eck (Region 8). Jim McNeeley also served as Director-at-Large, Membership.

At the 2019 Winter Meeting Rich Davis presented the revised "Convention Manual" to help future clubs sponsoring the convention. The board also approved pursuing the High Country/Boone Club to sponsor the 2020 Convention.

Conklin introduced the committee report on merging the election manual with the existing bylaws and removing the contradictions that resulted from the two documents being written at different times. Election processes and dates were now in one place. The committee agreed to make the changes requested and publish them in the next issue of *The Torch* for all members to read prior to the next convention.

The board also discussed a letter it had received from the Kalamazoo Club, the home club for former President Fink and former Executive Secretary Coppinger, questioning whether to continue its membership in the IATC. President Conklin responded to the issues raised in the Kalamazoo letter with an impassioned plea for them to reconsider leaving IATC that closed with these thoughts:

> What I'd like to leave you with is ... a sense of being part of a wonderful tradition, almost a hundred years old. When the Torch Club of Kalamazoo was founded, your city was just beginning to come into awareness of its important place in Michigan's economy. There was a new sense of preserving traditions built since Michigan became a state in 1837. Your club has formed an important part of Kalamazoo history—forging ties to other cities in your state—and ties to educated, professional people across the state and the US and Canada. The promise represented by Torch remains the same, today—a wonderful way to bridge the divisions which temporarily divide Americans.

In May the board continued its discussion of the bylaws amendments. The major issue was the qualifications for vice president. A motion was approved that the minimum requirements for the position remain as stated in the Torch "Election Manual": The candidate must have "held or is currently serving as an officer in a club; served or is currently serving as Regional Vice President; has attended at least one convention as a delegate; has been a Torch member for at least 5 years."

Anne Sterling and George Conklin (Durham, 2019)

Despite the efforts of Conklin and the IATC Board, the Kalamazoo Club voted unanimously to disaffiliate with the IATC effective June 1. Several other clubs dissolved in 2018-2019: Boulder, Columbia-Montour, Pennsylvania, Cincinnati, and Greater Rochester, New York. There were 1,938 members in June.

The 2019 Convention was held in Durham, North Carolina, hosted by the Durham/Chapel Hill Club. There were three panel discussions: "Helping Your Club Through the Use of Technology," "Public Water Quality," and "IATC Roles and Responsibilities." Papers included: "Artistry and Technology of Glass," "Public Broadcasting, Past, Present, and Future," and "Economics of Growing Up in a Mountain Community 1920-1960."

The Paxton Award winning paper was "Right to Free Speech" by Leland Robinson of the Frederick, Maryland, Club. According to Scott Stanfield, Robinson dazzled the audience with "his examination of political dialogue in the context of Buddhist teaching–an amazing intersection of the timely and the enduring."

OMG presented a draft of the budget for 2019-2020. Revenue was down due to a lower number of clubs and members. Actual dues revenue was $72,267.50 compared to a budget projection of $98,000. Based upon dues of $50 per member, that equaled a paid membership of under 1,500.

At this meeting the bylaws were amended to make clearer the nomination process, qualifications, and terms of office for regional director, president, and vice president. It added a detailed timeline for elections and contested elections.

Reed Taylor working even after retiring as the editor of *The Torch* (Durham 2019)

A tour of the Duke Lemur Center was offered. The center housed nearly 240 rare and endangered prosimian primates and constituted the world's largest and most diverse population of lemurs outside their native Madagascar. The attendees also visited the Sarah P. Duke Gardens. On Saturday there was a tour of the North Carolina Museum of Art in Raleigh.

July 2019-June 2020

President George Conklin began the second year of his two-year term. Dorothy Driskell, having served as interim vice president, was elected for a one-year term. Rich Davis would serve as treasurer and Anne Sterling would serve as past president. Elizabeth Short became the new Region 5 Director. Both Region 6 and Region 7 directorships were vacant. Sue Breen-Held joined the board as president of the Torch Foundation, replacing Anne Sterling.

In August Davis presented the year-end financial report for 2018-2019. IATC membership had decreased from 2,046 to 1,691, which created a significant drop in dues revenue. Davis stated that IATC could collect unpaid dues of approximately $5,000. The total revenue from dues could exceed $80,000. He noted that two-thirds of IATC funds went towards the management fee, $50,530 of $77,672.55 revenue. Whether or not IATC could afford to continue paying the management fee was discussed. Conklin suggested the board consider doing some management tasks itself in the future.

Richard Lynch, Gerald Stulc, and Timothy Spaeder at the Paxton Dinner

At the October 2019 Board Meeting, Conklin discussed additional roles for each board member to reduce the management fees paid to OMG. He appointed himself as webmaster. Tim Spaeder was appointed to review the database. Anne Sterling was appointed Club Manager/Secretary and Director at Large for Establishing New Clubs. Reed Taylor was elected as Director-at-Large of club Relations. Also, the board decided to include ten regional directors and four at-large members on the board. Proposed bylaw changes included removing the term "Executive Secretary" and replacing it throughout with various board member positions. The bylaws were to be presented at the June 2020 Convention for a vote.

The board asked OMG if the Torch webpage was searchable. The reply was that the webpage was based on an old database developed by Coppinger's firm and not all information could be updated. They said it would cost $1,500 to make the corrections needed and build a new page for the site. The board agreed to budget $2,000 for "Special Website Redesign."

Liz Short, Region 5 Director, declared there were issues that could not be fixed between IATC and OMG, and moved to give OMG 90-days' notice. She observed that the website and database had not been working for three years; Torch could no longer afford their services. Roger Kramer, Region 10 Director, disagreed, acknowledging there were some issues, but denying there was a crisis. Dick Lynch disagreed with terminating the OMG contract. He stated that OMG provided continuity, and IATC would lose that by changing management firms. No action was taken regarding the contract.

At the October 2019 Board Meeting a committee was appointed to review necessary services and later charged with conducting a bid process for a new management firm. The committee was co-chaired by Sue Breen-Held and Roger Kramer.

While plans were being made for the 2020 Convention in Boone, North Carolina. a novel disease swept across the world. In March, after more than 118,000 cases in 114 countries and 4,291 deaths, the World Health Organization declared COVID-19 a pandemic. States began to implement shutdowns in order to prevent the spread of the infection. Schools, universities, businesses, and clubs like Torch, ceased to meet in person. The world had changed! In his "President's Letter," Spring 2020, Conklin addressed the impact of the pandemic upon Torch, writing:

> For the first time since 1918, we are faced as a nation with a rapidly-spreading virus which makes us seriously ill. Not only have clubs canceled meetings for the rest of the year, but we are also asked to isolate ourselves from each other. State and national guidelines ask that groups be limited to only 10 people. So, for the first time since World War II, IATC has decided to cancel the convention.

The Boone, North Carolina, convention was postponed until June 2021 with the same program. Fortunately, the hotel did not penalize the IATC for the cancellation of the convention.

Although IATC did not hold a convention, it did hold an election remotely. Three individuals were nominated for vice president: Sue Breen-Held, then president of the Foundation, Rich Davis, the treasurer of IATC, and Roger Kramer, the director of Regions 7 and 9. Due to COVID-19, most clubs were not meeting in May, when the clubs normally discussed voting for officers in the IATC. A web page was developed to get information to members on the qualifications of the candidates for vice president, and to explain how the clubs needed to vote. Each club was asked to rank the three candidates for vice president, to elect the directors-at-large, to vote for or against the proposed bylaw changes, and then to mail or email the club ballot to the Elections Committee. Dorothy Driskell, as current vice president, would assume the position of president July 1, 2020.

The clubs approved a change in the bylaws to eliminate the requirement for an executive secretary. Conklin noted that while the board might engage professional help to handle some of the duties of running the IATC, most of the duties specified for an executive secretary would be handled by board members.

In May 2020 the board ended its relationship with OMG and contracted Outside the Cube Creative for one year to perform limited management and marketing services, including: database management for Torch Club membership; a monthly e-newsletter; website creation, support and maintenance; financial management such as dues collection; and *The Torch* design, layout, and publication. Outside the Cube Creative's management fees for 2020-2021 were budgeted to be $36,000, which was $14,000 less than OMG fees.

Based on financial statements of the IATC only $56,760 in dues revenue was received by June 2020. That equaled about 1,135 dues-paying members, though some clubs were not meeting or paying dues because of the pandemic.

The 2020 Paxton Award was given to Eric Davis for his paper "The Rapid Adoption of Artificial Intelligence: How AI is Changing Society and Culture."

July 2020-June 2021

Sue Breen-Held was elected vice president via the mail-in election procedure. Dorothy Driskell began her term as president. George Conklin became immediate past president. Walter van Eck served as secretary, Rich Davis as treasurer, and Scott Stanfield as editor of *The Torch*. In October van Eck was replaced by Gerald Stulc as secretary.

Outside the Cube Creative said a monthly e-newsletter had been launched with a new look. Rich Davis, Tim Spaeder, and Gerald Stulc noted that the change in the newsletter was well received. Outside the Cube Creative emphasized how important it was to have accurate membership lists from all clubs and wanted input from all of the regional directors.

At the July Board Meeting Treasurer Davis reported a net increase of $4,274.27 from dues received from the Worcester Club and the $3,500 Torch Foundation grant for magazine publication. He also presented the budget for 2020-2021 which included reduced management fees and publishing fees for *The Torch* due to the switch to Outside the Cube Creative. He noted that IATC assets totaled $103,000, including earmarked funds for conventions, member development, and the history project. He said a $5,419 year-to-date loss could be made up if the delinquent dues were paid. It was reported that the Hastings Club, the San Antonio Club, the South Hampton Roads Club, and the Fredericksburg Club would be paying their past dues. Davis noted that IATC had $96,000 in unallocated cash and about $71,000 in expenses annually to maintain membership lists, send out newsletters, keep an up-to-date website, and send out three magazines. He said IATC could survive this COVID year without any dues income, but could not survive on the remaining $25,000 for next year.

Conklin noted that many local clubs were not meeting because of state and local regulations banning in-person meetings. He suggested IATC develop a budget in the event clubs did not pay dues. Sterling said we should discuss how to offer value to members despite the pandemic. Breen-Held noted that the Foundation offered a grant to provide each club a free Zoom account. In August 2020 an all-member Torch Rally Zoom Meeting was held which everyone agreed was a success. It was decided that the rally be held quarterly and was renamed "Fireside Chat." By winter the majority of clubs were meeting and using Zoom. In fact, there was a potential of a new club starting using just the online meeting format.

Two of the most controversial events of the decade arose in September and lasted into the next year. One concerned a debate over the timing and political content of a paper for *The Torch* magazine. The other was an issue regarding registration of the Torch trademark.

In early September, in the review of the articles for the Fall 2020 issue of *The Torch,* leadership had concerns about one article. Because the article contained content critical of the Republican candidate for president, and the magazine issue would arrive shortly before the election, the president initially decided to remove the article. There were objections to this action, including from the editor, Scott Stanfield. Seeking a way forward, there was a discussion about delaying the article's publication to the winter issue after the election. When that solution was unacceptable to the editor and author, Vice President Sue Breen-Held led negotiations that resulted in the article being published in an edited fashion, with the content allegedly critical of the candidate included in a footnote at the end of the paper. A former board secretary was particularly disturbed by the alleged attempt to remove or postpone the publication of the paper. The degree to which he expressed his concerns to many, if not all, members of Torch troubled the majority of the board and many club members.

The second controversial issue, discussed at the September Board Meeting, was the status of the Torch trademark. The board was informed that the trademark was not registered, and the potential consequences included web providers taking down sites using a logo Torch didn't have rights for. Based on the estimated cost to hire an attorney to register the trademark, the board approved $2,000 to move forward.

In October, the board approved a resolution to form a committee to investigate allegations of misconduct by the former secretary. By November Jim Deegear of the San Antonio Club had been appointed chair of the investigating committee. He reported that Richard Lynch, past IATC President, would review *The Torch* article debate, and Dan Lundquist of the Saratoga Club would review other issues. At this point, the allegations regarding the former secretary's protestations about the magazine article seemed to be the most significant concern. However, it was soon overshadowed by the trademark issue.

An emergency board meeting was held on December 18, 2020, after the attorney on the trademark filing notified IATC earlier that week of a competing filing. That application for the registration of the official IATC trademark showed a former secretary claiming ownership as his own property on October 12. The filing had been discovered earlier that week. The board member had not notified the president, the board, or the management company that he had taken this action. When asked to explain the filing, the former secretary said he did it on direction from the past president (who had provided the filing fee), because they didn't think anyone was doing anything to protect the logo, despite the board decision in September to hire an attorney. However, the minutes indicated that he did not explain why he filed it in his own name rather than as an agent for IATC and why he did not inform any officers or the board for over two months, while claiming it was done "for the good of the organization." The following motion was made and seconded:

> It is resolved that whereas the Board of Directors of the IATC, Inc., in an emergency meeting duly called and attended for all requisite purposes, then considered and duly adopted the following: Whereas, a regional director of the IATC, Inc., has without authority or authorization caused to be filed on October 12, 2020 with the Commissioner for Trademarks of the United States, in his own name and as his own property, an official trade service mark, being fully described as application principal register for the registration of the official IATC mark, same being fully described in said application, and intentionally denominated as the property of the "owner of the mark."
>
> It is resolved that the board member is hereby immediately removed for cause as a director of the IATC, Inc., and from its board. He shall have no

authority of any kind or nature to act as such or in the name of the IATC, Inc. It is further resolved that this resolution be immediately transmitted to all Torch clubs.

The motion passed 8–3 with one abstention. Following the vote, the past president tendered his resignation from Torch. Dorothy Driskell accepted his resignation, with regret. Norine Haas filled his position on the board.

At the first meeting of the new year Davis reported that many clubs had financial difficulties due to the pandemic, with a significant number being inactive. The IATC budget benefited from having no convention in 2020, no board member travel expenses, and no expenses in December. A range of options was discussed regarding 2020-2021 dues, including deferring or decreasing dues for this year, and requesting the Torch Foundation's financial support for *The Torch* as an educational grant. Davis moved that along with the annual invoices, club treasurers be asked what they could budget for their dues.

In February, Stanfield retired as editor of *The Torch*. He thanked everyone for the honor and privilege of having served for eight years as editor. A Magazine Committee, chaired by Breen-Held, was formed of club members from six regions to review article guidelines, conduct a search for a new editor, and recommend action on both to the board.

Paul Scott Stanfield, Editor, *The Torch*

In this year the Stroudsburg, Pennsylvania, Muskegon, Michigan, Southeast Nebraska, and South Hampton Roads, Virginia, Clubs dissolved.

With COVID still a threat, the 2021 Convention was canceled but the Annual Meeting was held in June via zoom. There was a Paxton session to include the award winner and recognize the Gold and Silver Torch Awards, and a separate business meeting to include reporting on the IATC accomplishments, new board members, the new editor for *The Torch*, the vote on the new budget, plus membership, new clubs, and Foundation updates.

The Paxton Award was given to Judah Ginsberg for his paper "Consensus or Conflict." He earned a doctorate in American history and taught for several years at the Universities of Wisconsin and Illinois. He worked for several decades at CNN covering the State Department.

At the annual meeting Davis noted that IATC had a substantial bank balance but collection of dues was lagging. Outside the Cube Creative had covered some expenses. The cost of *The Torch* Spring and Summer issues had not been paid, and several other invoices remained outstanding, including legal fees for registration of the trademark for the color Torch logo. Davis recommended, as a last resort, to write off outstanding dues for several clubs still in arrears. The board approved.

The Torch Editor Search Committee members Bob Grogg and Elaine Kruse recommended Torch member Angela Dodson for the position. The board agreed and she accepted. Dodson had degrees in journalism and over forty years of experience in the communications field. In addition to recommending the new magazine editor, the committee submitted a report that included a job description for the editor which clarified the roles of the editor and publisher and guidelines for papers which were approved by the board for *The Torch*..

Angela Dodson (Current editor of *The Torch*)

President Dorothy Driskell and Vice President Sue Breen-Held continued to serve. Newly elected directors included Frank McCoy (Region 4), Dwight E. Williams (Region 6), Roland Zimany (Region 7), Art Bloom (Region 8), and Jim Deegear (Region 9).

At the July Board Meeting Rich Davis reported that the budget could not be balanced as the result of several factors, primarily because of outstanding unpaid dues from clubs. Only $31,000 in dues had been received by June 30 which equated to about 640 members. The budget had projected over $61,000 in dues or 1,235 members. Furthermore, various unanticipated expenses were incurred due to the early termination of OMG's contract, requiring Outside the Cube Creative to begin managing IATC sooner, including fees for setting up the website and activating licenses. The board approved a motion to recompense Outside the Cube Creative for the early transition expenses.

At the August Board meeting, Driskell named Norine Haas the new Nominating Committee Chair, and Leo Kellogg as chair of the Torch History Committee. At the same meeting, based on the report of the Investigation Committee regarding allegations of misconduct by a former board member, and allegations of improper interference with the editorial process with respect to the publication of *The Torch*, the board passed a resolution finding that the board member engaged in gross misconduct and abusive behavior, most prominently through multitudinous communications, and intentionally misappropriated the Torch logo. The former board member was censured and disbarred for life from all IATC offices or positions and from participation in any IATC-sponsored activities.

Regional Directors Tim Spaeder (Region 10) and Dwight Williams (Region 3)

A second resolution, concerning the past president, was passed regarding the allegation that he conspired in the misappropriation of the Torch logo. In consideration of his acceptance of responsibility and prompt resignation from the board he was censured and disbarred from holding any current or future office or position with the IATC for a period of five years.

With regard to the controversy arising from *The Torch* article, the Investigation Committee determined that no inappropriate interference occurred at any level in the publication of the article. What did happen was inadvertent communication problems resulting from a combination of factors: a new president, vice president, and management company, all unfamiliar with the then-existing publication process; the editor's historically prominent position in that process; a fast-approaching publication deadline; and an understandable, though perhaps over-zealous, effort to avoid perceived political overtones in the proposed article, coupled with a highly contested national election that would take place shortly after the magazine's planned publication date. Neither the editor nor the author felt that any perceived interference harmed the author's paper or message, though each professed a desire to clarify and strengthen the procedures vis-à-vis the executive, the editor, and the author. Regarding changes and edits to the article, not only did both the editor and the author profess to be comfortable with the give-and-take in the process, both were ultimately satisfied with the result.

Rich Davis, Diane (Dee) and Gerald Stulc

At the next meeting of the board in September, President Driskell allowed the past president to respond to his disciplinary action. He explained his decision to register the Torch trademark of his own accord. He agreed to reimburse IATC for the additional legal fees it incurred to research and register the trademark. He stated that his most valuable future contribution would be returning and contributing to his local club and keeping control of *The Torch* website, a site he controlled outside of the official Torch.org website which contained copies of articles from several years of *The Torch*. Furthermore, he agreed to disavow his relationship with the board member who received the lifetime ban. The board agreed to work toward a negotiated settlement with the past president to reduce his bar from service in an effort to bring unity to IATC and move on with its primary mission. Discussions with him continued through spring 2022.

In November Driskell announced a new Strategic Planning Committee to be chaired by Breen-Held. The aims of the committee were to recruit new members, retain existing members and clubs, and form new clubs. It was also announced that the Fall Edition of *The Torch* won the prestigious MarCom (Marketing Communications) Gold Award for excellence as part of an international competition.

Davis stated at the December 2022 Board Meeting that several more clubs had paid their past dues. Still, several clubs were in arrears, and a discussion ensued whether these clubs should be eligible for future mailings of *The Torch*. In January Davis noted that by comparison with midyear 2021, IATC was financially ahead. The Durham Club had paid their dues, and the Kearney Club hoped to pay. The Hastings Club was rebuilding. The Ft. Worth club was struggling, but planned to make a partial payment. Davis expressed hopes that enough 2021-2022 dues would be collected to achieve a financial balance. At the May Board Meeting Davis reported that half of the 2021-2022 dues had been collected. It was problematic to form a 2022-2023 budget based on current numbers. Expenses were increasing in part due to payment for Zoom licenses, updating and improvement of the data base by Outside the Cube Creative, and the increased cost of printing and mailing *The Torch* due to inflationary pressures. Grants from the Foundation requested for the 2022 Saratoga, New York, Convention and for expenses regarding publication and distribution of *The Torch* were approved. Breen-Held noted that there was nothing in the IATC budget to subsidize convention registration for the editor and co-editor, adding that stipends for registration be used. Authorization of $500 to subsidize the registration of *The Torch* was moved and approved.

Leo Kellogg had prepared an outline for the history project and applied for a grant from the Foundation to cover material expenses. He noted that a new Centennial History Project Team had been recruited and that Douglas Punger of the Winston-Salem Club and John Tordiff of the St. Catharines Club had agreed to serve as co-chairmen.

Doug Punger and John Tordiff, Century History Project Chairs

Art Bloom was nominated for the vice-presidential role. Haas reported that another member was interested in the candidacy for that office to be decided at the June 2022 convention, and this had the potential to lead to another contested election.

Lynn Bernard (Region 3 Director) and Art Bloom (IATC Vice President)

Two motions were submitted by email for a vote after the June board meeting: a motion to approve the final amendments to the bylaws, and a motion to rescind the ban on leadership participation by the past president. The latter was passed by the board following extensive discussion and correspondence with him and his reimbursement of additional legal costs. This put an end to one of the more challenging situations in this decade.

In Spring 2022, as the country and Torch were opening up after months of lockdowns due to the COVID-19 pandemic, there were 1,527 members in fifty-one active clubs. The average club size was thirty, with eight clubs having fewer than fifteen members.

The 2022 Convention was held in Saratoga Springs, New York. It was the first in-person convention in three years. Fifty-seven members and guests attended, representing twenty-five of the fifty active clubs. The meeting began with an evening reception at the home of Gerald Stulc. Among the papers presented were: "History of the Intersection of Art and Science in Representing the Human Body" by Stulc, "History of Saratoga Springs: Health, Horses and History" by Charles Kuenzel, "Six years a Hostage" by Terry Anderson, a former Associated Press journalist, and "Ulysses S. Grant and Grant College" by Grant College President Tim Welch.

Reed Taylor and Joe Zawicki on Lake George at the 2022 Convention

The gala banquet on Saturday night culminated events with an interesting and informative presentation by the Paxton Award winner, Professor Lowell Satre from the Youngstown, Ohio, Club, on "Coal Mining in Northern England in the 19th Century."

With regard to the proposed amendments to the bylaws, the consensus was that more time was required for everyone to review the changes. Therefore, the board agreed to hold a special convention in the fall to vote on them. A bylaws amendment was passed by the delegates to allow a bylaw approval vote to occur before the next convention.

July 2022-June 2023

Leadership passed to President Susan Breen-Held from the Des Moines, Iowa, Club. She was a consulting actuary in pensions for The Principal Financial Group for thirty-nine years. She served in several leadership positions in the Des Moines Club and the Torch Foundation. Art Bloom from Winston-Salem, North Carolina, was elected vice president in a contested election. Rich Davis, Tim Spaeder, and Anne Sterling were elected directors-at-large. New directors were Rod Gerwe (Region 8) and Joe Zawicki (Region 10). Secretary Gerald Stulc and Treasurer Rich Davis continued in their roles.

Art Bloom, Susan Breen-Held, Dorothy Driskell, Norine Haas, Anne Sterling, & Dick Lynch, current and past IATC Presidents (Saratoga, 2022)

Other appointments included Nominating Committee Chair Dorothy Driskell, Convention Committee Chair Rich Davis, Membership Committee Chair Tim Spaeder, New Club Development Committee Chairs Anne Sterling and Tim Spaeder, and Co-chairs of the Centennial History Project Doug Punger and John Tordiff.

At the August Board Meeting *The Torch* Editor Angela Dodson said a troubling trend was the decline not only in the writing quality but also in the number of papers being submitted. She said this might, in part, be attributed to the increasing use of PowerPoint rather than formally written presentations to clubs. It was clear to everyone that the board needed to proactively support the continuation of *The Torch* and encourage presenters to submit worthy papers to the editors.

Early in November Breen-Held undertook the first of several "listening trips," visiting eight clubs in Georgia, North and South Carolina, and Virginia. This outreach was done to help heal the divisions of the previous years and reduce the isolation imposed by COVID. She continued the visits in December with three clubs in Nebraska. The presidential listening tour continued in March with visits to five Region 2 clubs in Pennsylvania.

At a special delegates meeting in November a major revision of the bylaws was approved. Some former content was moved to a "Policies and Procedures Manual," including the election procedures. The new bylaws specified that board meetings were to be called by the president or upon written request by any four directors; monthly meetings were no longer required. Clubs remaining in arrears more than three months after receiving notice of that status were no longer considered to be in good standing. In addition, the bylaws included sections on disciplinary policies and a reduction in board size, along with new limits on the president's autonomy.

Ann and Joe Zawicki (Baltimore, 2023)

The 2023 Convention was held in Baltimore. The theme was "Legends Live Forever." Papers presented included: "Remembering John Hanson of Maryland, a Biography of the First President of the Original U.S. Government" by Peter Michael, from the Frederick, Maryland, Club; "Baltimore Maritime History" by Gerald Stulc; and "Wealth and Vision: The Nineteenth Century Contributions to Baltimore by George Peabody, Enoch Pratt, and William Walters" by Ann Weller Dahl. At the Thursday night dinner, members enjoyed "African Animals—The Joy of Discovery," an original film by Don Hobart.

Susan Breen-Held, Vice President, Dorothy Driskell, President (Saratoga, 2022)

Art Bloom discussed the launch of the Centennial Club, a fundraising campaign within the Torch Foundation for supporting established and new clubs.

Steve Sosson (2023 Convention Chair) and Susan Breen-Held

It was announced that a new club had been chartered in Williamsburg, Virginia. Two tour options were offered for Friday: the Baltimore Museum of Art and the Johns Hopkins Campus, or Fort McHenry and the Flag House. Saturday tour options included the Baltimore Aquarium, the Inner Harbor, and the Johns Hopkins Medical Campus; or the B&O Railroad Museum and the Babe Ruth Museum.

Scott Stanfield, former editor of *The Torch*, won the Paxton Award for his paper, "Stay in Your Lane: Who Gets to Tell the Stories of a Culture?"

Arthur and Louise Goldschmidt (2022 Convention)one hu

The persuasive arguments of Breen-Held and other members of the board convinced the membership at the June business meeting to increase the dues from $50 to $65, the first dues increase in fifteen years.

A Strategic Plan for the future of Strategic Plan" paragraph the IATC was presented by Vice President. Bloom. He discussed the launch of the Centennial Club, a restricted fund for supporting and establishing new clubs. A "Club Recruiting Resource Guide and Online Toolkit" was unveiled to help clubs recruit new members.

July 2023-June 2024

Leadership included President Sue Breen-Held, Past President Dorothy Driskell, Vice President Art Bloom, newly appointed Treasurer and Director-at-Large Paul Freiberg from the Fox Valley Club, and Secretary and Region 6 Director Dwight E. Williams. Other new directors included Ana Börger-Greco (Region 2), Steve Sosson (Region 3), David Coward (Region 4), Nancy Wardwell (Region 5), Barbara Harrington (Region 7), Rod Gerwe (Region 8), Luke Daum (Region 9), and Torch Foundation President Pat Shutterly.

Presidential listening tours resumed in October, with visits to the eleven clubs in Regions 1 and 10, a group covering three states and Canada. December saw visits to our two clubs in Texas (Region 9). Recruiting and club growth continued to be important topics to the clubs.

In January 2024 the Lima, Ohio, Club surrendered its charter but the remaining eight members converted to "members-at-large." In February Anne Weller Dahl was pleased to report that she had recruited a number of people to form a new club in Townson, Maryland. In the Spring of 2024 the Chambersburg, PA club dissolved.

The Winter 2024 edition of *The Torch* contained three articles that some readers considered politically partisan; they did not hesitate to say so. In response, the board announced that it would consider potential policy changes regarding publishing Torch articles on current political issues and involve members in shaping them, to ensure the policy respected all viewpoints. Members were invited to complete an online survey. The board aimed to strike a balance that respected the diverse perspectives of our membership.

Liz Teufel & Evan Thomas, editors, *Sharing the Light*

The 2024 Convention was held in Richmond, Virginia.

Tours included the City of Richmond, the Black History and Valentine Museums, Virginia Museums of Fine Arts and History and Culture, and the Virginia State Capitol.

As the International Association of Torch Clubs ended this decade and its hundredth year, its membership had rebounded somewhat from the depths of the pandemic to 1,468 members in about fifty clubs. It is hoped and believed that the future is bright for Torch as it strives in multiple locations to form new clubs, increase membership, and maintain its existence as a forum for reasoned discourse.

Chapter 6: The Torch Foundation

A Tale of One Foundation with Three "Lives"

The Origins and First Decades

Written by Ann Weller Dahl
Researched by Nancy Wardwell, Paul Scott Stanfield, Stephen Toy, and Rich Davis

In the same year that the International Association of Torch Clubs celebrated its fiftieth birthday, a proposal was put forth in a June 3, 1974 letter to the officers and directors, by the IATC's Director of Development, A. Vernon Davis of the Hagerstown, Maryland, Torch Club. He proposed an organization that would expand the IATC's reach, while never diminishing the founding principles of Torch. He sought the formation of a Torch Foundation. This is the story of its realization and accomplishments. As with any organization, the Foundation's basic structure and specific goals have changed with the passage of time, but today Davis's idea is still an important segment of the IATC's overall structure. As Davis wrote:

> The Association needs to visibly show that it cares about promoting and extending Society's opportunities for advancement through inter-disciplinary, inter-professional approaches to problems, issues and opportunities that forever confront Society.... Operating in the public service field, the Torch Foundation would include among its purposes the sponsorship of research, educational, and promotional programs intended to encourage inter-disciplinary, inter-professional discussion, study and communication of the problems, issues and opportunities confronting Society.... As in the Association itself, the Torch Foundation would encourage and assist free exploration of any issue or question of general interest, but in no way endorse any course of action on matters of political, social, economic, or religious concern, or any candidate for public office.

Initially, Davis envisioned several undertakings:
- Promote a pilot program of undergraduate and graduate inter-disciplinary, inter-professional discussion, study, and communication.
- Expand the content and promotion of *The Torch* magazine.
- Establish fellowships.
- Produce and distribute publications and films.
- Support lectures and seminars.
- Establish approaches to the problems confronting Society.

The letter concludes that "it would be helpful to have direction from the [IATC] Board of Directors."

Figuring Out How to Establish Such a Foundation

Establishing a Torch Foundation proved to be a lengthy process. Two years passed between Davis's proposal and the next archived letter, dated July 27, 1976. Written by Thomas L. Carroll of the Lincoln, Nebraska, Torch Club, it was addressed to Forrest M. "Frosty" Smith, Jr., then President of the IATC and a member of the San Antonio Torch Club. Several issues were addressed in Carroll's letter, among them the operating needs of the IATC itself, where to find start-up money for the Foundation, and whether or not this proposed Foundation could be tax-exempt. Carroll suggested that if the gift were tax-deductible, and the cause deemed worthy, then giving would increase substantially. He urged that solicitations be made using a figure that would make the appeal worthwhile—a $100 request, not a paltry $5. He discussed the topic of tax considerations, saying that under the present idea of a "charity" the Foundation really would not qualify. He had, however, a wise solution to that problem: "But we could, I believe, create a nonprofit corporation which would be qualified to receive tax deductible gifts, if the corporation is established clearly for educational purposes." Carroll tackled next what the money collected could be used for, under the "education" guideline: It could create a Torch Fellowship Program, which would pay one year's membership in a local Torch Club to outstanding students on a professional track. He saw this as a way to attract young men to Torch. He also saw such a program as answering the question of "What does the IATC do for us except send the magazine?" Referring to Davis's 1974 proposal, Carroll agreed that such a Foundation could expand the magazine's content and promotion. Support of the magazine is still a function of the Foundation.

In support of creating the Foundation several committees were formed by the IATC Board. One, under the leadership of Vice President Clifton Rodgers, was named the Committee of Resource Advisors and consisted of Torch members who were familiar with legal and financial operations relating to the organization of such an entity as the Foundation. The members were Thomas M. Barney from Buffalo, New York; J. L Cohen from Stroudsburg, Pennsylvania; David C. Eaton from Harrisburg, Pennsylvania; Robert N. Perry from Harrisburg; Robert S. Rosow from San Antonio; and John P. Vitko from St. Paul, Minnesota.

An Organizational Committee was tasked with incorporating the Foundation and soliciting contributions. Members present were Forrest M. Smith, Jr., Chairman, Arthur I. Palmer, Jr., Douglas M. Knudson, Clifton E. Rodgers, and Fred R. Whaley, Jr. Financial support was tested among a group of IATC past presidents at the Long Beach, California, Convention. A majority pledged $100 toward the organizational expenses of the Foundation. Among that group were Chairman Leo G. Glasser, Norman P. Crawford, Harry J. Krusz, James S. Owens, W. Norris Paxton, and Nelson R. Torbet.

In the summer of 1976, in a letter to Carroll, Vice President Palmer of the IATC, who was also an attorney, reminded him that Torch would probably have to set up a separate fund to receive money for educational purposes, which funds would not be used to supplement the general budget. He further opined that he doubted that collecting money for this new Foundation would be easy, since there were some members who even balked at the idea of paying the $10 Torch dues! At the January 1977 Board meeting Palmer stated that if only a meager $10 were expected from each member, then there was no need to create a 501(c)(3) corporation. However, for $1,000 donations a 501(c)(3) status would be needed.

June 1977 brought much excitement because the annual convention was to be held on the Queen Mary, docked at Long Beach. It also brought encouraging news about the Foundation. On June 21 the Director of Region 2, Clifton E. Rodgers, outlined to IATC Board members a plan for doing some groundwork about a Foundation before the July Convention and even listed people from each region to serve. This action had come about from a request made by Smith that Rodgers investigate the successful foundations already established by Rotary and the American Society of Landscape Architects. In July a memo from Editor Lee Hoffman noted that the draft of an organization plan "gives the Board and Staff some basic guidelines for serious consideration." Rodgers's letter ended with an assignment for the board: Please fill in the "yes" or "no" answers to a series of questions from the Resource Advisors. It seemed that it might become necessary, though expensive, to engage a qualified attorney to write up a "fully developed organization plan and by-laws."

Rodgers wrote to President Palmer on September 24, 1977, following up on the convention's decision that the establishment of the Foundation was "to have a high priority with the Special Projects Committee." He thanked the Committee of Resource Advisors who had "functioned with unanimous enthusiasm favoring the Foundation," and invited each of them to serve on the *ad hoc* Committee of Advisors. He noted the positive response to the aforementioned questionnaire, saying that it "gives the International Association of Torch Clubs an affirmative position to move ahead with organization of the Foundation." Rodgers mentioned the folks who had already pledged an initial contribution of $100, should the 501(c)(3) status be granted.

He listed steps to be taken in organizing the Foundation, authorized by the Organization Committee at Long Beach:

- Explore the advantages or disadvantages of setting up a Delaware Corporation versus a Minnesota Corporation.
- Create a flyer about the Organization Plan and a Pledge Card to promote the Foundation.
- Prepare a letter inviting individual clubs to become a Friend of the Torch Foundation.
- Send a letter to each Torch member with the plan and an invitation to become a Fellow or Sustaining Member of the Foundation.

Looking ahead, Rodgers anticipated introducing the Foundation's plans at the 1978 Convention in Hershey.

The Organization Plan

It was not until November 1977 that a third revision of an organization plan for the proposed Torch Foundation was submitted. It echoed and expanded on the original that had been proposed by Davis three years before. The plan was quite detailed.

I. Purpose

As in Davis's 1974 proposal, this organization would reflect the importance of "the interchange of knowledge between recognized professions" and "further the educational goals in the arts, sciences, and humanities" of tomorrow's leaders.

II. Administration

The size and power of the governing board were specified as follows:
- The board would have fifteen trustees, being careful to avoid having the same people serving on both the IATC and the Foundation Boards.
- These trustees would be chosen by the IATC Board, five each year.
- Three trustees would be past presidents of the IATC; each of the ten Regions of the IATC must have a representative on the Foundation Board.
- The only compensation to board members would be for travel expenses.

III. The Goals of the Foundation

The immediate goals for 1977-1978:
- Incorporate the Foundation.
- Solicit $20,000 to establish a modest investment account before the annual convention.
- Work further on the organizational plan.
- Establish the benefits that the Foundation would offer to Torch members.
- The long-range (ten year) goals were: (1) Be worth one million dollars and (2) Solicit $125,000 per year.

IV. The Mission of the Foundation

The authors of the Plan saw the Foundation giving a whole new dimension to Torch, the opportunity for members to share in a program which would do these things:
- Provide financial assistance to worthy young men and women for the purpose of an education and self-improvement.
- Break down the barriers between professions.
- Enlarge the boundaries of knowledge in all professions.
- Promote good will between people and nations of all races, creeds, and religions.

V. Activities

The organization would be empowered to do these things: Solicit funds to

- Provide scholarships and fellowships,
- Endow or establish professorships,
- Assist in research projects, and
- Provide dissemination of information through publications, exhibitions, lectures, and seminars.

VI. Qualifications for Foundation Awards

The following recommendations were made:

- Very specific criteria would determine the selection of awardees at the undergraduate, graduate, and professorial levels.
- There would also be scholarships available for people wishing to have technical training.
- Highly qualified people already working in a profession could attend seminars or pursue a research project. These experiences would last for four to eight weeks. Likewise, highly qualified professional people could attend a local Torch Club and the annual convention for a period of one year.

VII. Awardees

The following rules were established:

- The regional directors would call for applicants, form a committee to interview the candidates, and then send their recommendations to the Trustees of the Torch Foundation for the final selection.
- Relatives of Torch Foundation Trustees were not eligible to win an award.
- One award would be made per Torch region. Generous clubs or regions might give more than one award.

VIII. *The Torch*

It was felt that tax-deductible gifts to the Foundation would make it eligible "to subsidize all or part of the cost of publication."

IX. Categories of giving

- Fellow—A Torch member or non-member who has contributed or in whose honor a contribution of $1,000 has been made in one year.
- Sustaining Member—A Torch member or non-member who has contributed $100 per year and intends to make regular contributions. After ten such donations the donor would become a Fellow.
- Memorial Certificate—Given to the donor of $100 or more, with the deceased person's name on it.
- A Friend of The Foundation—"Recognition by certificate to each Torch Club which adopts the practice of contributing annually a minimum of $10 for each new member admitted during the preceding year, plus $1 per year for each member in the Club."
- The Torch Foundation may be named by a member or non-member as the beneficiary of a will or a life insurance policy.
- The Trustees "may arrange for special grants and gifts from individuals, foundations, corporations, and government agencies."

Launching the New Foundation

On May 21, 1979, the Torch Foundation was incorporated pursuant to the laws of Delaware. The Articles of Incorporation indicated that it was formed exclusively for charitable and educational purposes: (1) to fund the Paxton Lecture Award; (2) to publish and disseminate outstanding Torch lectures; (3) to award scholarships to students under the Torch Fellows Programs.

According to the proposed Foundation organization plan, set forth in November 1977, the first Foundation Board would have consisted of fifteen trustees representing different groups within the IATC, with no member of the IATC Board also serving on the Foundation Board, if at all possible. Each year the IATC Board would appoint five new trustees. Unfortunately, information in the archives contains no information about the first Foundation Board. It can safely be assumed that the first president was Forrest M. Smith, Jr.

The Foundation's proposed areas of interest and service required a considerable amount of capital. To that end President Smith of the Foundation distributed two letters soliciting pledges from other IATC veteran members. One of these was addressed to a general audience, as "Dear Friend in Torch," while the other was sent to an individual with not only typed information but handwritten comments. Smith, in a June 1979 letter, wrote:

> You are among the ever-growing number of persons who hold a special place in your mind and heart for Torch.... Now Torch has a baby! Derived from seminal discussions and promptings during the five years a concept has arisen extending the influence of Torch to a separate non-profit corporation known as the Torch Foundation. Taking the core theme of Torch itself-professional excellence-this new foundation is dedicated to enhance the achievement of professional excellence and ethics in every occupation....

The first public presentation of the new foundation will be made at the Torch convention in Norfolk, June 17-20, 1979. This letter represents the first private presentation of the foundation (which has recently been incorporated in the State of Delaware.) I'm contacting a number of veteran Torch members, such as yourself, prior to the Norfolk Convention to ask you to make a preliminary pledge toward the new Foundation. Our tax-exempt status will be assured after August 1, 1979, so either post-date your checks or send them after Lammastide! [Lammastide was a harvest festival celebrated by the Celts between the summer solstice and the fall equinox.]

Smith went on to list the various categories for giving and the fact that groups, as well as individuals, Torch members and non-members alike, were eligible to contribute. The money could be designated "in memory of" or "in honor of" groups and individuals and could also come from stipulations in wills, bequests, and legacies.

At about the same time Smith sent a much shorter letter designed to get the same result—a pledge toward funding the new Foundation. This one went to Carroll and expressed the hope that the assorted pledges, made before the June 1979 Convention in Norfolk, Virginia, would spark generous giving among the attendees. Smith advised Carroll to make his pledge now but to withhold his check until notification that the Foundation was eligible to be tax-exempt.

As it turned out, Carroll had to wait quite a while before making his pledge good. It was not until December 1980 that the IRS letter was received granting the Foundation tax-exempt status. With that significant hurdle now passed, Smith tried again to solicit funds. His April 19, 1981 letter was cosigned by Secretary Robert S. Rosow:

Dear Friend in Torch:

What we hoped would take only a few short months has turned into a year and a half—but all of us have been patient and compliant and at last we have it—our tax exempt status! The Torch Foundation will be officially launched at the Torch Convention in Washington June 3-6, but we're approaching all the special Torch members who made pledges during our Norfolk campaign, asking them if they will again consider their generous pledges and help us make up for lost time....

... To seed the foundation we are planning to ask each Torch member to come forth with a very professional $100 (paid either at once or quarterly over a year) establishing each as a Founding Fellow of the Foundation.

Smith wrote another letter addressed to the Board of Trustees of the Foundation on June 2, the day before the 1981 Washington Convention convened. It updated the board on the amount of money pledged before, during, and after the 1979 Norfolk Convention: $3,190.51. It added that the Foundation would be introduced to the Washington Convention during the business session.

On June 28, 1982, after the convention in Knoxville, Tennessee, IATC President Elect C. A. Peterson of the Columbus, Ohio, Torch Club sent a letter to the directors of the Association.

It noted that in the rush to finish convention business, the request from the Foundation "for reaffirmation by the IATC Board of a position of support in principle by IATC of the Foundation" had been overlooked. Enclosed was a letter of an affirmation written by Smith:

Be it hereby resolved:

- That insofar as the Torch Foundation involves individual Torch Clubs in implementing the Foundation's plans and purposes, full communication and approval of the methods to be used will be obtained in advance from the IATC Board or its Executive Committee. To this end an IATC board member will be appointed by that board to serve as liaison with the Foundation.

- That after such approval has been obtained, the advice and full cooperation of the officers and board members of the IATC will be provided and gratefully received by the Torch Foundation in pursuance and implementation of the Foundation's program.

Torch Position on Politics Put to the Test

In a letter apparently written between April 19 and May 19, 1981, Foundation President Smith wrote this to the President of the United States:

Dear President Reagan:

Most of us professionals are so pleased with the renewed image you are giving the Presidency that we in the private sector want to do everything we can possibly do to support you. With you as a person with a high-profile professional image we shall be launching June 3-6 in Washington a new foundation dedicated to building the professional image in America. Its name will be the Torch Foundation.

We have devised a unique solution—at least a partial solution— to many of the social ills that beset this country—such as crime, welfare, abortion. Our solution would save the government billions of dollars each year. It would cost the government nothing for it would come from the private sector. It could cause one of the most spectacular social advances in this nation's history. It would be of personal interest to you because this solution could serve as an effective deterrent to such persons as John W. Hinckley, Jr.

I have written enough, I hope, to interest you. What I am requesting is a personal interview to explain what I mean...

Was this letter overstepping the bounds that the IATC had always placed on presentations, discussions, and involvement? Carroll definitely thought so. On May 19, 1981, he wrote a carefully composed letter to Smith, saying:

It is my fervent hope that what I am about to write will not do any permanent damage to our long and well-founded friendship.... But I must tell you that I found reading your "letter to the President" in behalf of the Foundation.... the most flagrant violation of the basic tenets of Torch I have found in the entire history of our Association....

Torch, as we all know, was built by generations of men who were dedicated to the proposition that above all Torch must at all times remain free of commitment to political causes.

The fact that you spoke as an official of the Foundation and not the Association is quite beside the point. The rank and file of our membership is not going to make any distinction in philosophical policy between one and the other.... I know of the intensity of your dedication to Torch.... I hope that this aberration from our time-honored policy can soon be forgotten and that it will never happen again.

Apparently Carroll sent copies of this letter to the Foundation trustees and officers. In a June 2, 1981 letter to the Foundation Trustees, Smith addressed the topic of his letter to President Reagan. He said, "I regret any misunderstanding my letter may have generated. Let me assure you that the Torch Foundation, its aims, its programs, its personnel, and its approach are strictly a-political."

Crisis and Rebirth of the Foundation

In the mid-1980s the controversy over Smith's letter to President Reagan was overshadowed by a dispute with him over the mission of the Foundation. As president of the Foundation, Smith was concerned that the Judeo-Christian principles on which America had been founded were no longer respected by today's youth. In a letter published in *The Torchlight* of August 1985, he proposed that the Foundation become involved in a program to assist youth in promoting high ethical standards, called Preventive Operational Neurolinguistic Therapy (PONT). At least one local club disagreed with the program's objectives.

At the IATC Board meeting in Richmond on June 29, 1986 two concerns about the Foundation were discussed: (1) The Foundation had not been operating "in line with its original intent, which was funding The Torch Magazine." (2) The relationship between Smith and the IATC itself was unclear. It was further noted that the Foundation operated with the blessing of the IATC. This statement, backed up with the negative issues previously mentioned, seems to have been cause enough for the IATC to decide to "recapture" the Foundation. In doing so, the board would name new trustees. IATC President Robert S. Rosow volunteered to ask Smith and the trustees for their resignations.

President Rosow opened the July 1, 1986 IATC Board meeting with a brief statement about the history of the Foundation. Then Peterson reported on his and Rosow's June 30th meeting with Smith, where the action of the IATC Board was conveyed to him. Smith was informed that he could either resign as president or the IATC Board would pass a motion to sever sponsorship of the Foundation. He could remain as a trustee with the appointment of four new trustees satisfactory to IATC. Smith "met this action with some resistance." Rosow would begin a search for four new trustees who would be responsive to the Foundation's needs.

An August 1987 article in *The Torchlight* relayed several important announcements made at the Akron, Ohio, Convention, just past. President Rosow announced that all the Foundation trustees had resigned and that new trustees had been elected. Reorganization of the Foundation was now complete. The first "life" of the Foundation had ended.

Meanwhile a capital campaign had been initiated, to be chaired by Richard Rosen, to collect $60,000 over a three-year period, 10 percent of which had already been pledged by the IATC directors and officers. Two priorities were announced for the use of this money: "the Torch Foundation would guarantee the quality, maintenance, and enhancement of *The Torch*" and "the Foundation would eventually embark on a program to sponsor lectures and scholarships." The Foundation also hoped to extend the magazine's distribution to libraries and educational institutions and to provide a stipend for the Paxton Award.

Paul Stanfield, one of the five new Foundation trustees, devoted his usual "P.S." column in the December 1987 issue of *The Torchlight* to the Foundation. Trustees Dick Rosen, Art Palmer, and Stanfield attended a meeting in the fall at which they hoped to map out the Foundation's plan of action, before realizing it just couldn't be done so quickly. Three officers were elected by the trustees to serve one year terms: President Clarence Peterson, Vice President Dick Rosen, and Secretary/Treasurer Paul Stanfield. Bob Glasser participated as an advisor. The Foundation's income would serve two purposes: to enhance *The Torch* and to continue to support the Paxton Award.

Saginaw, Michigan, was the site of the 1988 Convention. Leading up to it were several IATC Board meetings. At one in January 1988, it was announced that 10 percent of the money for the capital Foundation campaign had already been pledged. At the June 17 meeting it was announced that Peterson was now the president of the Foundation and that John Suchy had assumed the jobs of secretary and executive director.

The 1990s

At the February 13, 1991, IATC Board's teleconference, the members were brought up-to-date on the Foundation. IATC President George Crepeau reported that he was working toward reviving interest in the Foundation. To this end an article for *The Torchlight* would be prepared by the Foundation President Peterson. Crepeau would also mention the Foundation in his article, and at the upcoming convention in Buffalo there would be a presentation on the Foundation.

An information sheet about the Foundation was given to delegates at the 1991 Buffalo Convention. The Winter 1992 issue of *The Torchlight* carried a first-page article by Foundation President Peterson titled "It's Time to Reactivate the Foundation." He was honest about the organization's less-than-stellar history: The basic problem seems to have been to shape an initial objective for the Torch Foundation sufficiently broad as to have an appeal to a wide spectrum of Torch members who would be called upon to support the Foundation financially.

Peterson spoke of the recurring debate about the relationship between the IATC and the Foundation, which had continued throughout more than a decade. This difference of opinion had resulted in waning interest in the Foundation, followed by the board's withdrawal of its initial approval of then-president Smith's PONT plan and the request that Smith and the trustees resign.

Peterson's article closed with details about the current objective of the Foundation: "to build an endowment fund through gifts and bequests from Torch members." He noted that at the present time its assets were just over $4,000, and it needed $20,000 "to ensure the income level necessary to pay its corporate franchise fee and to underwrite the Paxton Award each year." The hope was that the endowment would grow to a point that several other projects could be undertaken.

On June 26 at the 1992 Convention in Columbus, Peterson presented a financial report and the Foundation's plan for the future. He asked each delegate to tell their local club about the Foundation, and asked each regional director to appoint a "contact person" to the Foundation in each club. He reminded everyone that the donations were tax-deductible.

The following September 27 a statement was made at a board meeting concerning the feasibility of programs related to the Foundation. The idea of soliciting donations from outside Torch was discussed.

At the 1993 Portland, Maine, Convention Crepeau announced a proposal set forth by Peterson and Crepeau, dealing with a project to be undertaken specifically by the Foundation, according to Peterson something that had "the potential to truly fan the flame of Torch." The new project was based on a 1991 document titled "The Torch Foundation—Directions for the 1990s and Beyond." It specified three areas in which the Foundation would support the work of the IATC: continuing to support the Paxton and Editor's Quill awards, investigating methods for supporting these awards, and establishing scholarships to be awarded to children or grandchildren of Torch members. Beginning at the 1994 Norfolk Convention two scholarships would be awarded, one for $1,500 and another for $1,000. The new project was presented out of serious concern for the future of the IATC and the hope of invigorating the Torch experience. The Foundation had the funds to support the project for the next three years. Beyond that donations would need to be forthcoming, or the Foundation would need to dissolve.

At the 1994 Convention Crepeau announced the Foundation's balance as $12,257.24. Peterson had resigned, so the board requested that Crepeau become the Foundation's president. The board also approved a motion that the Foundation president become a non-voting, *ex officio* member of the IATC Board. Crepeau reported that the Foundation wanted to fund one issue of *The Torch* and wanted any surplus money from conventions to go to the Foundation. Outgoing IATC President Richard R. Lynch remarked that the relationship between the IATC and the Foundation was closer than in the past.

In its Spring 1995 issue *The Torchlight* carried a front-page article by Crepeau, addressing what he saw as a "win–win opportunity—The Torch Foundation. He wrote:

> the Foundation is dedicated to the support of special activities of The International Association of Torch Clubs and [serves] as the vehicle through which individuals and Clubs are able to make gifts and bequests....

> ... To that end the trustees (the five immediate past presidents of the IATC), with deep, committed and serious concern for the future of Torch and the Torch experience, and in the belief that efforts of the Foundation may help re-invigorate Torch, ask that Torch Club members and Torch Clubs with financial surpluses consider contributions to the Foundation.

The IATC Board meeting on October 1, 1995, featured a more detailed financial report of the Foundation than in the past. The balance on hand as of May 1995 was $12,257.24. Treasurer Suchy had placed $8,000 in a thirty-month certificate with a yield of 6.314 percent. With the remaining $4,448.06 the Paxton Award was supported, and $114 spent to have a tape made of the Paxton Lecture. A request was made for money from the board to support the duplication of four more tapes for the regional directors. It was suggested that the original tape be retained by the Foundation. One copy should go to the Paxton lecturer and one to Norfolk, which had hosted the 1994 Convention. The other copies could be shared by the regional directors.

At the Fall 1996 Board meeting Foundation President Crepeau reported that at the Chicago Convention the Foundation treasury stood at $12,225. While in Chicago he had collected $2,500.

Three years later, at the Fall 1999 Board meeting, Crepeau proposed that the back cover of *The Torch* be dedicated to the Foundation. "It would list the names of the people who make donations in memory of a member, give recognition of donors, and explain how and why one should give to the Torch Foundation." He also requested "an examination of the process used to arrive at the Paxton winner." He felt that recent papers had not been up to the desired quality and wanted an evaluation form created to determine if a submission was a good Torch paper.

And so, the 1990s ended, having illustrated variations on three themes that had been present since the organization's conception in 1974: What should be the activities of the Foundation? How could the Foundation get money to support those activities? And, What, exactly, was the Foundation's relationship to the IATC?

Bringing the Second "Life" of the Foundation to a Close

Ever since the idea of a Torch Foundation was conceived and then incorporated during the mid-to-late 1970s, only four people had been in the leadership position: Forrest M. Smith, Jr., Clarence Peterson, George Crepeau, and beginning in 2004, Ralph Falconer. Smith, Peterson,

Crepeau, and Falconer had all previously served as IATC presidents. With varying degrees of success, but always with enthusiasm and dedication, each president tried to bring to fruition the lofty and oft-changing goals of the Foundation, which were aimed at supporting the work of the IATC, its parent organization. To that end, each president had attempted to raise the necessary tax-deductible funds and to accumulate income from the Foundation's investments.

Moving into the twenty-first century, it became clear that the Foundation was uncomfortably less than a stable, successful organization. An October 4, 2003 letter from Foundation President Crepeau to IATC President Thomas J. Bird revealed that all was not well:

> Changes must be made in the structure, the policies, and the procedures of The Torch Foundation.... The approach to developing such changes calls first, for a complete "re-thinking" of the idea of a foundation.... The positive and optimistic purpose of this exercise is for the IATC to find and describe a possible future for the Torch Foundation and if it is found that there is a future, to create an appropriate structure to support that future.

To the letter Crepeau attached a detailed plan titled "The Torch Foundation: Finding the Future/ Funding the Future." It was to be presented at the IATC Board meeting in Norfolk two days later. Subtitled "An Outline of an Investigation," the plan suggested forming an *ad hoc* committee of the board "to explore all opportunities made possible at this critical period in the history of the Torch Foundation and its relationship to the International Association of Torch Clubs." It was divided into sections headed Options, Requisites, Recommendation, Timeline, Next Steps, and Notification. Especially catching the reader's eye was the last of the five options: "If all fails to resolve the critical situation facing the Foundation, it could be prudent to consider a dissolution of The Torch Foundation."

Crepeau wished that the final decision concerning the Foundation's future be made at the 2004 Convention in Wilkes-Barre, Pennsylvania. The option of dissolution was not chosen. After Crepeau relinquished the presidency, he was followed by Ralph Falconer of the Akron, Ohio, Club.

A lengthy letter was written by Falconer to the IATC board for the 2006 Convention in Bethlehem, Pennsylvania. In it Falconer discussed how he was managing the finances of the Foundation, how much he anticipated the investments' values would increase in a relatively short period of time, and what could be done for the IATC with those funds. He noted that the amounts were, by then, considerably higher than when he had assumed the presidency. While his ideas sounded hopeful, their wisdom remained to be seen. He wrote:

> The main attention recently has been trying to grow the principal through online investing.... The amount invested was $20,000. Through short-term investing this principal grew to over $30,000 in early June.... There is an expectation that this asset value will continue to grow. Fortunately, this growth will enable use of the Foundation in ways that we have not seen before.... If we can count on the principal doubling each year, we can take up to $10,000 or more from the principal each year. I think that will be possible and that will enable

us to do attractive things for Torch that will capture attention and get more donations from Torch members.

Falconer continued with some creative ideas for *The Torch* and hopes for a better financial future. His ideas included publishing a larger, more colorful magazine with features that would make the publication more attractive. He also called for increasing support of the website. These would attract more Foundation members and donations.

Richmond, Virginia, welcomed the 2007 Convention, a year when that state was celebrating the 400th Anniversary of the Jamestown settlement. Falconer was unable to attend, so Secretary Jack Horner, who was also entitled to buy/sell investments, gave the Foundation's report. No funds had been received since the 2006 Convention, and the values of the investments were down. He was unaware of what had happened to a memorial donation of $120 from the Youngstown Club. An auditor had reviewed the books, which were fine, but had never submitted a written report. Annual disbursements included the $25 franchise fee to Delaware where the Foundation was registered, $275 for the required resident oversight, and $250 for the Paxton winner, plus the cost of the trophy. Several board members commented on the report and made suggestions for actions requiring the Foundation's immediate attention: IATC President Anne Sterling opined that the board should receive regular reports from the Foundation. Dick Lynch pointed out that the Foundation had "no clear role" and recommended that it "develop an objective to solicit funds or they should consider closing the Foundation."

The Foundation Board, such as it was, met on October 28, 2007. Tom Bird was present; Falconer and Horner were both officers and trustees. Crepeau was absent. Sterling had been pulled in as an *ex officio* member. Falconer stated that some Foundation Board members had expressed concern over the method he used to invest the funds and had recommended specific changes. He related that Sue Breen-Held, a trustee, disagreed with his method and had resigned over this. Her objection was that he had been trading in short-term investments online because he believed that "one needs to act quickly." Breen-Held felt strongly that Foundation investments, unlike personal investments, should be made for the long term and be diversified, perhaps using stop-loss orders to save gains.

Foundation Secretary Horner mentioned that the existing bylaws needed to be updated. Region 1 director Charles Carlson "questioned if the Foundation is worth the effort for the small amount of money they have." Falconer requested that the IATC Board give him additional time to resolve the issues mentioned in his report, and promised a full report at the Lancaster Convention the next year.

Falconer's Foundation report in 2008 was not unlike his reports from years past: The original $20,000 had fluctuated in value with the market (no current value was mentioned); the bylaws needed to be revised; the membership was still small and paid dues of only $5 annually. He recommended that prospective members not have to be approved by the Foundation Board because they were already IATC members. At the conclusion of the meeting a motion was approved commending the work of Horner and Falconer and requesting that they remain on the Foundation Board.

The repeatedly unsteady situation with the Foundation soon produced a confrontation. On May 2, 2008, Sterling, soon to be the past president of the IATC, wrote a confidential, very perceptive memo to incoming president Stephen Toy, and Jimmy Strickland, Torch's Executive Director. The memo reported on "our current problems with the Torch Foundation, as I see them." The memo listed concerns about the Foundation president, who (1) denied access to the Scottrade brokerage statements to the Foundation or the IATC Board members; (2) divulged only verbally any financial reports, using "approximate" values; (3) refused to reveal the specific equities held; (4) consulted no one on his board before buying or selling equities, nor revealed the results; (5) did not mention consulting a financial advisor, if he had one. Another area of concern for Sterling involved the absence of specific actions that should have been part of such an organization's operations. There were no minutes of meetings. A contribution sent by one club upon a member's death was not acknowledged. It was not clear who, exactly, was on the Foundation's board. No effort was made to update the bylaws or increase membership. There was no recognition that mismanagement of the Foundation reflected badly on the IATC. Sterling concluded her memo with these words, using the third person instead of her name:

> The current IATC president has tried to use persuasion, rather than confrontation, to get the Foundation to follow its by-laws. At present, the best hope is to make sure that members at the June 2008 convention are encouraged to join the Foundation by paying dues. This would provide a body of members, at last, and they would be authorized to vote for a responsive Foundation board.

The opening paragraph of the June 28, 2008 minutes of the Foundation's Annual Membership Meeting (mistakenly labeled the Board of Trustees Annual Meeting) contained a rather strange sentence concerning the day's agenda: According to President Falconer, no agenda had been established for the meeting, and comments or suggestions from those present would be welcomed. The section of the minutes listing the current officers and trustees, some of whom were filling two roles, illustrated again the need to follow the bylaws, and indeed to revise them. The assembled Foundation members, a number of whom had just paid their $5 to join, voted on a new Board of Trustees. Elected were Richard (Dick) Lynch, Tom Bird, Jerald Radice, Walter van Eck, and Ann Dahl. Their terms were for one year. Falconer agreed to turn over the books. Bird gave a brief history of the Foundation. Following this was an updated financial report given by Treasurer Jack Horner which was critical of Falconer's management of the Foundation's finances:

> Money was transferred to Ralph Falconer who is the investment person.... Falconer invested the rest of the funds in shares in a financial company that insures municipal bonds. This was the wrong time to do this because of a decline in the market. The funds did fall below $20,000. Ralph is unable to give an exact figure. The shares that Ralph bought were over $1 apiece and he bought 16,000 shares. The [independent] investment advisors at the time were suggesting that the price of the shares would go as high as $3 a share.

The final discussion dealt with a new and extremely important issue: the Oldenburg Trust of almost $58,000 bequeathed to "the I.A.T.C. Endowment Fund" by the will of the late Robert A. Oldenburg of the Chicago Torch Club. President Elect Toy pointed out that the Foundation's Board of Trustees would need to approve a resolution accepting this bequest.

In a detailed, no-nonsense memo to Foundation President Falconer, IATC President Toy listed two requests made by the board at their November 2, 2008, meeting. They wanted to see "(1) the Torch Foundation's Financial Activities and Status and (2) a Road Map for Future IATC-Foundation Cooperation."

Toy continued:

> The first part of this request, the request for past financial records, should be straight forward. The IATC Board should have a detailed accounting of the handling of Foundation assets. As president of the IATC, I have a moral, and perhaps legal, obligation to account for the assets donated by our members to the Foundation. It is not my intent to publish these records for all to see; however, if requested by any member of the IATC or Foundation, these records should be made available to them. After all, it is their money.
>
> The second part of this letter is a proposed road map to insure good will and support between the IATC and the Torch Foundation. The IATC's endorsement is essential for the Torch Foundation's support and survival. In order to have the IATC's full support, the Torch Foundation needs to remain true to its founding documents, namely its own by-laws and certificate of incorporation.

While acknowledging that some progress had been achieved in Lancaster the previous June, Toy listed six items that the Foundation still needed to act upon:

- Membership retention and expansion
- Appointment of an Executive Director
- Announcement of the upcoming annual meeting in Appleton
- Establishment of a time and meeting room for the annual meeting
- Preparation of financial reports and minutes of the 2008 annual meeting for distribution at the 2009 Appleton meeting
- Decisions regarding the Oldenburg Trust

Toy's memo closed with these words: "The time has come to bite the sour apple and repair many years of neglect the Torch Foundation has endured, and you have inherited. I know all of you personally, and I know every one of you wants only the best for the IATC and for the Foundation. Working together, we will achieve our goal. Ignoring the problems, we will not."

At the February 3, 2009 Board meeting, Falconer admitted that he had been depressed because stock had been sold without his knowledge, adding that had the sale been delayed for just a few weeks, the profit would have been much higher. Another long report concerned the Oldenburg Trust. A troublesome sentence was about the tax status of the Foundation.

Falconer said he needed to obtain a letter from the IRS stating that the Foundation was, indeed, a 501(c)(3) organization. Also discussed was where the Oldenburg money should be housed.

After the passage of nearly a year the trustees felt inadequate progress had been made by the officers of the Foundation in addressing the deficiencies outlined by IATC Presidents Sterling and Toy. Further, there was little progress increasing the transparency of operations of the Foundation. At the urging of the IATC presidents, and pursuant to the bylaws of the Foundation, trustees called upon Foundation President Falconer to convene a special meeting of the trustees specifically to enlarge the voting membership of the Foundation. With the reluctant agreement of Falconer, a special meeting of the trustees of the Foundation was called to order on June 26, 2009 at 8 a.m., prior to the scheduled meetings of the membership of the Foundation. The minutes of the meeting indicated that before the meeting "a number of new members completed a membership application and paid the required dues...." Further, "A motion was made, seconded, and unanimously passed to accept the applicants as members of the Foundation." Thereupon, "A motion to adjourn was made, seconded and passed unanimously." That was the only business conducted at the special meeting of the trustees.

Ann Dahl, Ed Latimer, Walter van Eck, Steve Toy, Anne Sterling (Richard Lynch Absent)

Minutes show that immediately thereafter, the regular membership meeting of the Foundation was called to order by Falconer. His financial report at the Convention listed approximately $1,000 in the checking account, approximately $14,000 in a Scottrade account, and a check from the Oldenburg Trust. He announced that the next annual meeting would be at the 2010 Convention hosted by the Youngstown Torch Club. In due course, the President called for election of new trustees for the Foundation. The successful nominees for trustees were Richard R. Lynch, Stephen T. Toy, Edward B. Latimer, Thomas Bird, and Ann Weller Dahl.

At 8:30 a.m. on June 26, 2009, the regular meeting of the Foundation Board of Trustees was called to order by President Falconer. All the newly elected trustees were present. After the routine approval of the minutes of the last regular meeting of the trustees, the president called for the election of new officers of the Foundation. Walter van Eck was nominated for president, Ann Weller Dahl was nominated for vice president, and Richard R. Lynch was nominated for secretary and treasurer. No other nominations were made. Thereupon, the officers were elected unanimously by the trustees.

The gavel of power passed. The coup had succeeded!!

Amid jubilation, President van Eck and the other officers assumed their respective duties. Sterling and Toy deserve the gratitude of the entire IATC membership for skillfully mobilizing volunteers to resolve the crisis in the Foundation and return it to institutional health. Thus ended the second "life" of the Foundation and the beginning of the third. This "third life's" tale was in sharp contrast to those of the first two.

The Recent Era, 2010-2024

Written by Richard R. Lynch

2010

On June 26 a motion to re-elect the existing Foundation trustees was passed by the membership. Van Eck announced that $13,165.75 would be the second and final installment of the Oldenburg bequest. Despite the efforts of Toy and Lynch, little progress had been made on correcting the Employer Identification Number (EIN) and tax-exempt status. Lynch recommended that no new investment opportunities, other than certificates of deposit, be considered, since verification of EINs typically was required to establish new investment accounts, and the Foundation could not provide that verification.

Van Eck and Fischer agreed to develop templates to facilitate contributions to the Foundation. Van Eck agreed to work on a newsletter. Lynch agreed to solicit membership renewals. Fischer discussed the need for an expenditure and investment policy. Van Eck agreed to compile a record of past transactions and to inform the trustees of steps necessary to equitably resolve problems and to keep the board informed. Sterling emphasized the importance of transparency in Foundation operations, including publication of meeting dates and minutes.

On June 16 a special telephone meeting of the Foundation Board was convened by President van Eck. It was the first-ever telephone meeting of the trustees. The purpose of the meeting was to prepare for the upcoming Hagerstown membership and trustee meetings. The officers, President van Eck, Vice President Dahl, and Secretary/Treasurer Lynch, were re-elected to office for the upcoming year. It was agreed that any members desiring to participate in the 2011 membership meeting must pay the new dues amount of $25 in that calendar year. Proposed expenditures for the Foundation were discussed, emphasizing the need to observe both the IRS and the Oldenburg Trust restrictions on expenditures.

The proposed topics for discussion at the upcoming convention membership meeting included the successful reinvigoration of the Board of Trustees, the routine conduct of Foundation business in an open and forthright manner, the resolution of the recent IRS Tax Levy (which was rescinded, after numerous, long, and painful conversations between the Foundation President and IRS officials), the final distribution of the balance of the Oldenburg Trust, and the anticipated confirmation of the Foundation's EIN and tax exempt status.

At a Foundation meeting on June 25, Toy congratulated Crepeau for finding the elusive IRS letter dated December 1980 granting the EIN to the Foundation in the IATC archives at The Ohio State University. The importance of this discovery can hardly be overstated. It confirmed the tax-exempt status of the Foundation and solidified the ongoing ability of the Foundation to accept tax deductible contributions. Much celebration ensued!

The existing officers were routinely re-elected. Lynch reported that the checkbook balance of $5,092.50 was reconciled to the latest bank statement. He also reported on the income and expenditures for the year, and stated that the Foundation's Money Market balance was $50,359.68 as of June 10, 2011. The treasurer's report was accepted with appreciation for its completeness and accuracy.

There was discussion of ways to publicize the Foundation and encourage memberships. Francis Moul's proposal to establish lifetime Foundation memberships at $500 was discussed.

On August 5 van Eck called a special telephone meeting. Concerns were expressed about reimbursing officer and trustee expenses, prompting a call for development of a policy on reimbursement. Van Eck proposed that the annual IATC convention could be contracted to the Foundation. Its sales tax exemption could significantly reduce the costs of the convention.

Under the direction of van Eck, Dahl, Lynch, and the new trustees, management of the Foundation was dramatically improved. Agendas were developed and distributed before meetings, minutes and treasurer reports were promptly distributed, corrected, and approved. The trustee vacancy precipitated by the resignation of Robert Fischer was filled by former IATC President Anne Sterling. A "Sconce" award was established for those clubs which met Foundation membership goals. The decision was made to deposit the revenue from Lifetime memberships into the endowment, and to use only the income resulting for ongoing operations. The Oldenburg bequest finally made programming and future significant accomplishments of the Foundation a realistic possibility. A genuine excitement about growing the Foundation to a maturity it had not enjoyed previously was palpable!

Despite the enthusiasm of the Foundation executives, impediments to smooth operations surfaced. Inaccurate local club information frustrated the goal of increasing Foundation membership. Loss of records by the IRS was especially discouraging. The IATC Board was unwilling to transfer the Convention Fund to the Foundation, a prerequisite to using the Foundation's tax-exempt status to reduce the cost of conventions.

The establishment of an investment policy for the Foundation was a major decision. Lynch suggested that criteria for selection of an investment vehicle include (1) past performance, (2) least onerous restrictions on the availability of funds, and (3) lowest investment cost.

The board considered investment in a community foundation. Upon further investigation it was discovered that in effect, the Torch Foundation would need to "gift" its funds for investment to the community foundation, and that the community foundation would have the authority, upon request, to distribute Foundation "gifts" to the Foundation, *or deny such requests.* After considerable research and discussion, the board decided not to use a community foundation for its investments.

After discounting the community foundation investment vehicle, there were further discussions of potential investments for Foundation funds not needed for immediate expenditure, and for seeking professional investment guidance. After extensive and animated discussion by the officers and trustees, professional investment guidance was foregone, and upon motion of Treasurer Lynch, investment of the total amount of the Oldenburg bequest not needed for immediate expenditure was invested in the T. Rowe Price New Horizons Mutual Fund with E-Trade Brokers.

2012

At the next regular meeting of the trustees on January 12, 2012, the following lengthy motion was unanimously passed:

> The Board of Trustees of the Torch Foundation declares the following: by investing the proceeds of the Robert A. Oldenburg trust bequest, we will not be creating a new trust, but simply a restricted endowment fund, within the overall endowment funds the Torch Foundation will be holding. We accepted the Oldenburg bequest from the Oldenburg Trust but now that the bequest is in our hands, the money is no longer part of a trust, but will become simply the Oldenburg Endowment Fund. This Oldenburg investment line must be kept separate—forever. Former IATC President Toy and former Torch Foundation President Falconer signed legal documents to that effect. Accordingly, it was decided, with this initial investment of the Oldenburg money, to invest the exact sum of the bequest in one vehicle. The value of that investment may fluctuate or be reinvested in one or more different vehicles in the future. It

may do better—or worse than other foundation investments but from now on it's a separate ship, sailing on its own. Foundation trustees will have the power to use the income for the Oldenburg Endowment Fund's limited purposes. However, the trustees may never henceforth commingle any of the principal—be it larger or smaller—with other Foundation money. The Oldenburg Endowment Fund we are about to create will represent a commitment to keep those funds separate from all other foundation funds so that the income may be properly utilized for the limited purposes specified in the request, namely "... to supplement the existing information service to members and prospective members." (See Page 4, Item 5 of Charitable Share Schedule No.1, Robert A. Oldenburg Trust). This commitment must be maintained by future Foundation Trustees.

Following up on prior discussions establishing Lifetime Foundation Membership, Torch Foundation Certificate of Lifetime Membership Number 0001 was presented to Francis Moul.

During 2012 regular meetings were held and significant progress made. However, frustrating delays were experienced in opening the Foundation's E-Trade account. The need to develop an annual fiscal year budget was discussed. Bylaws were amended to allow independent financial advisors to be hired. Sterling broached the concept of establishing a Foundation Grant Program. Bylaws were amended to prevent a person from simultaneously holding the positions of Foundation president and secretary. A total of thirty-eight Foundation members, including ten Lifetime and eight new annual members, was reported. Douglas reviewed financial records from 2009 to 2012 and reported them to be in good order. The Foundation's accomplishments included confirmation of the EIN number and tax-exempt status of the Foundation, ability to use PayPal, trustee term limits, updates to the web page, and moves toward finalization of the E-Trade account. All in all, a good year for the Foundation!

In June 2012 Trustees van Eck, Lynch, Dahl, Toy, and Latimer were elected. At the subsequent trustee meeting, officers elected were President Anne Sterling, Vice President Stephen Toy, Secretary Ann Dahl, and Treasurer Richard Lynch.

2013

On June 20 the annual Foundation membership meeting was held in St. Catharines, Ontario. Sterling presented an optimistic "State of the Foundation" report: The Foundation had made enormous strides since its reorganization in 2009. Assets had grown from about $20,000 to about $90,000. She noted that the sole purpose of the Foundation was to be of use to the IATC, its parent organization. The Foundation now operated in a transparent manner. The Foundation's income was being used to make grants to several Torch Clubs for various purposes and also to purchase Directors and Officers Liability Insurance, to encourage participation on the board by offering basic financial protection. Donors could take advantage of the Foundation's 501(c)(3) tax-deductible status when making contributions to the New Clubs

Initiative. Sterling concluded that the greatest asset of the Foundation was the officers and trustees themselves.

2014

In June Sterling said she would be stepping down as Foundation President due to her responsibilities as the president of the League of Women Voters of Virginia. Lynch reported in detail on the assets of the Foundation. Toy discussed the grant program offered by the Foundation. Latimer presented a brief history of the Foundation. Trustees elected were Joseph Vincent of Lehigh Valley, Pennsylvania, Harry Hinrichs of Des Moines, Iowa, Stephen Toy of Newark, Delaware, Edward Latimer of Columbia, South Carolina, and Walter van Eck of Portsmouth, Virginia. The newly revised bylaws required the election of trustees for staggered terms, so some would serve for one year and others for two. At the Foundation Board meeting Lynch was elected president. Trustee and Vice President Toy and Secretary Dahl were re-elected. The treasurer position was vacant.

In August Lynch introduced Susan Breen-Held of the Des Moines Club. Her background eminently qualified her for treasurer, and she was elected unanimously. There was a discussion of how to establish a person in each Torch Club to represent and promote the Foundation. Dahl agreed to work on establishing a list of those who could fulfill this new role. There was a request by Moul that the Foundation pay the $5,450 cost of the Fall 2014 issue of *The Torch,* using money from the Oldenburg Fund. Discussion of the fund guidelines followed. A grant for an issue of the magazine was approved.

It was suggested that the archives at Ohio State, where records of the IATC were stored, be used as a repository for records of the Foundation.

Dick Lynch, Anne Sterling, Stephen Toy, Ed Latimer (St. Catharines, 2014)

2015

The year started off on an optimistic note, with active participation of all the trustees and officers. Breen-Held indicated the membership totaled forty-three, including fifteen lifetime members, six in the process of becoming lifetime members, and twenty-two annual members. The total value of the Foundation on December 13, 2014 was $102,693.53. There was jubilation since the Foundation assets had, for the first time, exceeded $100,000. A wide-ranging discussion of investment strategy followed. Van Eck and Breen-Held played major roles in the development of the complicated procedure which would restrict expenditures from the endowment to assure its continuation in good times and bad.

At the trustee meeting following the June 2015 Convention, Vincent relinquished his trusteeship because of work commitments, and Marlene Cupp, Anne Sterling, and Ed Latimer were elected as trustees for a three-year term.

Important achievements for the year included: authorizing the development of a manual by Leo Kellogg to capture the important policy decisions approved by the trustees; compiling a budget for the 2015-2016 fiscal year; obtaining renewal of Directors and Officers Liability Insurance; continuing discussion of appropriate investment vehicles for the Foundation; approving reimbursement to Moul for costs related to the establishment of the Fredericksburg, Virginia, Club; approving a grant to the Westminster, Maryland, Club to host a regional meeting; and developing an easily understood financial format by Treasurer Breen-Held. The active engagement, cooperative attitude, and the desire on the part of the executives of the Foundation to function in a completely transparent manner was remarkable. It led to the adoption of a detailed, four-page investment policy at the last meeting of the year. The formalization of this policy was a significant achievement.

2016

At the beginning of the year, the increasing complexity of operations of the Foundation became evident. An accounting software package was acquired. Progress in adopting business-like practices for the Foundation continued unabated during the year.

The Foundation's investments had shown reliable growth, but the significant retreat in the market prompted an animated discussion relating to whether the Foundation should convert some or all New Horizons holdings to cash. Patience in relation to the performance of the market was urged, and no actions were taken.

Moul's $1,000 and Toy's $500 contributions to the New Clubs Initiative were celebrated in recognition of the founding of the new Saratoga, New York, Club. Sterling was asked to be chair of a new Memorial and Honor Roll Program.

At the 2016 Convention new Foundation Trustees George Conklin and Maxine Moul were welcomed by existing trustees Sterling, Cupp, and Latimer. Reelected were President Lynch, Vice President Toy, Secretary Dahl, and Treasurer Breen-Held.

2017

By the beginning of 2017 it became obvious that the IATC was facing financial troubles, largely due to a decrease in membership and dues income. It seemed that the long-term solution would be the formation of new clubs and increasing membership in existing clubs. The short-term solution could be a grant from the Foundation. After considerable discussion two motions were approved unanimously: (1) that the Foundation give a grant of up to $9,000 to support the educational aspects of the IATC budget from March 1 to June 30, 2017, and (2) that the Foundation request more transparency and communication with the IATC so that the Foundation could be aware of the progress being made on the formation of new Torch Clubs and the reinvigoration of existing clubs. There was discussion of $4,100 sent in December of 2016 to the IATC in support of the development director. The end-of-year Foundation asset balance exceeded $160,000.

At the Kalamazoo Convention the Foundation membership elected three trustees, Leo Kellogg, Ed Latimer, and Susan Breen-Held, to serve with continuing Trustees Conklin and Moul. The trustees elected President Anne Sterling, Vice President Dick Lynch, and reelected Secretary Ann Dahl. The treasurer position remained vacant.

Former Treasurer Breen-Held was thanked for her excellent work. Shirley Eberly of the Rochester, New York, Club was nominated for that position. Sterling told of Eberly's background as Treasurer of the League of Women Voters of the United States. Eberly added that she and her husband had been Torch members since 2008, and that she had served as the Rochester, New York Club's president, treasurer, and newsletter editor. She was elected unanimously as Torch Foundation treasurer.

2018

Despite financial concerns of the IATC, the Foundation confidently continued under the leadership of Sterling. The need for a communications officer became increasingly critical to accomplish the twin objectives of spreading the good news of the Foundation's achievements and increasing Foundation membership among IATC members. Sterling challenged the executives to suggest ways to reach the $200,000 target set for the Foundation.

After some discussion the following statements were adopted:

Mission Statement

To support educational activities throughout the International Association of Torch Clubs to develop opportunities and recognition that encourage lifelong learning, reasoned discussion, and interchange of information between Torch members.

Vision Statement

Ongoing support for a strong, continuing community of professionals who share their strengths and passions in good fellowship.

2019

Sterling convened a "Committee of the Whole" to identify likely candidates for upcoming vacancies in both trustee and officer positions. Plans were made to contact all IATC members to inform them of the existence of the Foundation and to acquaint them with its good works and achievements, in the hope that at least a few would volunteer for upcoming officer and trustee positions. Plans were also made to update, publish, and distribute the Foundation brochure.

Following the Foundation membership meeting in Durham, North Carolina, Sterling called a meeting of the trustees. She welcomed new trustees Dave Hammond of Columbus, Ohio, Peter Dowling of Saratoga, New York, and Roland Moy of Boone, North Carolina. Officers elected were President Sue Breen-Held of the Des Moines, Iowa, Club, Vice President John Tordiff of the St. Catharines, Ontario, Club, Secretary James Johnson of the Lincoln, Nebraska, Club, Treasurer Shirley Eberly of the Rochester, New York, Club, and Communications Officer John Fockler of the Youngstown, Ohio, Club.

Anne Sterling conducting a Torch Foundation Meeting (2019)

Plans were discussed to publish a letter from President Breen-Held in the next issue of *The Torch*, including a bind-in envelope, to encourage new membership in the Foundation and to increase contributions. Plans were made to update the Foundation's brochure and widely distribute it to all IATC members. Hammond agreed to explore storage of Foundation documents at The Ohio State University Archives. The treasurer reported that the Foundation's investments continued to do well. Trustee Lynch gave a brief financial report, saying that the Foundation was currently valued at just under $174,000.

2020

The impending appearance of a Foundation page on IATC's website was eagerly awaited. A study of money market investments was undertaken. Hammond and Lynch developed a records retention schedule which was ready for review by the executives of the Foundation.

Although the nation was beginning to recognize the invasion of COVID-19, no one at this time really appreciated the far-reaching impact the epidemic would have on all gatherings, including those of Torch members. Regular meetings continued to be held by phone. Beginning in April visual meetings were begun on Free Conference Call. Being able to see all participants in the meeting was a huge improvement over aural-only communication. By May plans to hold the IATC Convention had been cancelled, and many were disappointed by the dashed prospect of seeing their friends. Nevertheless, convention grant applications were received, reviewed, and awarded, with the proviso that the grant could be "rolled-over" to the following convention.

Peter Dowling of the Saratoga, New York, Club and Roland Moy of the Boone, North Carolina, Club, were selected as trustees at the annual membership meeting. Officers elected by the trustees included President Sue Breen-Held, Vice President John Tordiff, Secretary Jim Johnson, Treasurer Shirley Eberly, and Communications Officer Dan Looker. Subsequently, Tordiff resigned as Vice President of the Foundation for health reasons.

Treasurer Eberly called for a formal review of investments held by the Foundation to see if they were still appropriate in the current financial climate. She reported that assets totaled over $216,000, more than doubling since December 2014.

2021

With the resignation of John Tordiff the office of vice president remained vacant. Nonetheless, the regular business of the Foundation continued.

Since the epidemic again forced the cancellation of the annual IATC Convention, the customary membership meeting and the following trustee meeting were held online in 2021. At the annual membership meeting Breen-Held reported on the healthy nature of the Foundation. Hammond, Dahl, and Latimer were elected as trustees.

At the meeting of the trustees officers elected were President Richard R. Lynch, Vice President Patricia Shutterly, Secretary James Johnson, Treasurer Shirley Eberly, and

Communications Officer Daniel Looker. There was discussion of informing members that retired people with an individual retirement account could avoid taxation on donations made to the Foundation from their required minimum distribution.

On August 29 President Lynch communicated that he was unable to continue in office for "medical and personal reasons." Fortunately, Pat Shutterly, a very able and experienced vice president, agreed to accede to the presidency. Once again, the office of vice president was vacant, but fortunately on November 12 Sandy Stewart was appointed to fill the vacancy.

2022

The year began with great excitement in anticipation of an annual convention in Saratoga, New York, the first in two years. This was tempered by the sudden and unexpected resignation of capable and well-respected trustee Dave Hammond for health reasons. At the January meeting of the Foundation Dick Lynch was welcomed back as a trustee. At the Foundation's Annual Membership Meeting in June Pete Dowling and Roland Moy were re-elected as trustees to serve two-year terms ending in 2024. The current officers were re-elected to serve another year.

2023

The Foundation executives met after the beginning of the new year. The willingness of the executives to meet regularly was a tribute to them and an acknowledgement of their commitment to the goals and objectives of the Foundation. Everyone appreciated the camaraderie and easy working relationship that existed among the group. Dan Looker retired as the communications officer. In a vote of confidence in the president, a motion was passed that the formulation of the agenda ought to be an executive responsibility, not one the trustees needed to approve. A budget committee was appointed, composed of Dowling and Eberly, consulting with IATC Treasurer Rich Davis, to ascertain IATC priorities for the year. Eberly reported that Foundation assets had totaled about $188,000 at the end of November 2022. A Foundation budget in the amount of $23,500 for the new fiscal year was approved. It addressed the highest priorities of the IATC and was supported by the Foundation trustees. It included $8,000 support for *The Torch*, $5,000 for convention activities, and $6,000 for convention grants.

In the midst of these discussions a concern arose: it appeared that many, even long time IATC members, had little or no knowledge of the Torch Foundation. As a novel way to bring new IATC members awareness of the Foundation and the good work it does, they discussed creating a new Honorary or Aspiring Foundation Membership category. These members would pay no dues for their first year but would receive regular information about the Foundation.

Since they would be better acquainted with the Foundation, they would be more likely to join the next year.

Trustees Dowling and Moy and Secretary Johnson were enlisted as a Nominating Committee to select candidates for three trustee vacancies to be voted on by the membership at the convention.

A Foundation meeting was held in March. The convention chair of the IATC attended and requested $5,000 to help defray educational activities associated with the convention. Much discussion ensued, particularly concerning the precedent-setting commitment. The grant was approved after reassurances that each year's grant request would be subject to approval and based on the financial status of the Foundation. During the spring of the year, Douglas Punger was elected communications officer for the Foundation.

A major new IATC initiative to provide funds for increasing membership in existing clubs and to provide support for founding new clubs, was discussed. The initiative, to be known as the Centennial Club, would rely on the donations forwarded to the Foundation so that they would be tax-deductible and available to the IATC as expansion grants. IATC Vice President Art Bloom discussed plans for the Centennial Club, indicating that its goal would be to raise $100,000 in five years. This money would all be used to increase existing club membership and to fund aggressive new club initiatives. There was concern that a Centennial Program, residing in the Foundation but publicized by and benefiting IATC, could confuse potential contributors to other Foundation programs, such as the Honor and Memorial Programs. Treasurer Eberly reported that the Honor and Memorial recognition program had amassed more than $19,000 in unrestricted funds.

Marshall Marcus, Pat Shutterly (Foundation President), Rod Gerwe (Saratoga, 2022)

In advance of the 2023 Baltimore Convention, the Foundation Convention Grants Committee announced awards to the St. Catharines, Blue Ridge/Leesburg, Virginia, Richmond and Westminster, Maryland, Clubs.

At the Foundation Membership Meeting Lynch, Dahl, and newcomer Violet Meek were elected as trustees. The trustees appointed President Pat Shutterly, Vice President Douglas Punger, Treasurer Shirley Eberly, Secretary Jim Johnson, and Communications Officer Anne A. Thomas. Resigning her vice president position, Sandy Stewart was thanked for her convivial participation in Foundation deliberations. Trustee Edward B. Latimer, quite possibly the Torch member with the longest record of participation in the activities of both the IATC and the Foundation, was profoundly and warmly thanked for his unmatched commitment of over seventy years of service.

Following a detailed effort to review, clarify, and consolidate the bylaws, an amended version was distributed and approved.

In an exciting prelude to an unveiling at the convention, IATC President Breen-Held presented the Foundation executives with a description and illustration of the IATC "Toolkit," a step-by-step outline and templates to help local clubs organize critical activities and increase membership.

Eberly reported that as of May 31 the balance in the T. Rowe Price New Horizons Fund had grown to $168,399.93. Trustees approved the diversification of investments by authorizing investment in the T. Rowe Price Growth fund. As of September 30, 2023, total assets of the Foundation exceeded $208,000!

And so, in its third "lifetime," the Foundation is healthy and strong. The capable management and routine operation of the Foundation are a testament to its executives and their willingness to fulfill their obligations in a professional, straightforward, and transparent manner. Meetings are open to all members of the Foundation, to interested IATC members, and others. Foundation executives look forward to meetings and appreciate the cordial relationships experienced in accomplishing their responsibilities. The future of the Foundation is bright.

Chapter 7: Flicker or Flame: The Future of the IATC

By Arthur L. Bloom, Vice President

> A rock pile ceases to be a pile of rocks the moment a single man con-
> templates it, bearing within him the image of a cathedral.
>
> – Antoine de Saint-Exupery

The mass of the rock pile stands tall. For one hundred years men and women have added to its height and weight, labored singly and in devoted groups to place boulder upon boulder. Others guided the selection from the large pile of rocks those that could best be hewn and set in place. The scale of the foundation remains vast. Walls loom heavenward. The builders over five generations have given portions of their lives to the construction of all that exists. Their blood and sweat can be found in the mortar that unites stone to stone. Many of those devoted laborers have died since the building project began. Their work remains unfinished. What now of the present generation of builders? Do they continue to envision the cathedral that gives meaning to the rocks before them, or have they lost their sense of collective steward-ship of this century old project?

I am neither architect nor contractor. I am but the mixer of mortar and the holder of the trowel. What shall we do with the questions we face regarding what we are building, how we should be building it, and why building it even matters? At the launch of The International Association of Torch Club's Centennial year my hope remains that we, like many before us, will embrace the vision of something glorious.

As Scott Stanfield at the beginning of this book wisely stated:

> As with any organization one hundred years old, changes in leadership have
> created an institution somewhat different from that which Bullock proposed
> in 1924. But over generations the *raison d'etre* has remained the same: the ex-
> change of ideas among professionals.

I agree with Stanfield that all things change. As original visions meet the anvil of reality, time and shifting ideologies act like hammers shaping the metal of all institutions. Many break as a consequence of this pummeling. Torch endures, but a century of hammering has rendered it vulnerable. Torch still exists to foster the exchange of ideas, but we lack an organization-wide consensus regarding which ideas are worthy of exchange and which ones should be rel-egated to the realm of personal opinion. Each Torch Club has its own perspectives-on such matters. As an organization of diverse Torch Clubs, the IATC is committed to fostering har-mony among members and assuring that its actions and services build community among all our clubs. Absent meticulous care for the whole, factionalism endangers the mission of the IATC. This we cannot allow.

Many of the factors weakening the foundation of Torch are not new. The need to lower the aggregate age of the membership, for example, has bedeviled Torch for decades. As organizations age through time, so does their membership. Of the nearly 400 members who responded to the 2023 all-member survey, 80 percent of the respondents were seventy years old or older and 42 percent were over eighty. Aging brings with it the benefits of wisdom and experience, and for many, time to engage in productive pursuits. But as we also know, age can sap our energies, calcify our thinking, and shift our perspective away from the future and toward the past.

The Board of Directors engaged recently in discussion of the strengths and weaknesses of Torch and the factors that stand to have a corrosive impact on the organization's future. Assets include:

- One hundred years of history and experience
- The robust new website and IATC's award-winning magazine
- Use of technology to increase interaction among members
- Member satisfaction levels with their local clubs
- Rising trust levels as the IATC Board demonstrates greater transparency and effectiveness in addressing long-term problems
- An approved strategic plan with measurable goals and objectives

Contrast these strengths with the following weaknesses:

- The rising age of the membership, which now exceeds an average of seventy-five
- Exceedingly limited involvement of local members in the activities of IATC
- The dearth of submission of articles for publication *The Torch*
- Insufficient resources at the IATC level to meet rising demand from local clubs for support in recruitment and retention of members and for other needed services

Add to these the following challenges:

- Insufficient financial resources to achieve long-term financial sustainability
- Rapid decline in membership
- Economic volatility limiting willingness of members to accept dues increases
- Diminishing numbers of members who are able and willing to accept leadership roles
- Diminishing social cohesion reflected in the weakening of voluntary associations like Torch

For IATC to survive, change must occur. Financial and management issues must be addressed. Membership needs to grow. Can IATC deliver sufficient value to its member clubs to warrant the continuation of its existence? If IATC fails to embrace an inspired and inspiring vision for its future, it will perish. This is not an indictment of our present volunteers, but a clarion call for all Torch members as we move into the future. I am asking whether we, as members of the local Torch Clubs that comprise IATC, have within us the capacity to dream as our organizational founders once dreamed. It seems that at present the work of the IATC is incidental to the life of the local clubs. No organization ever survives if it is unwilling to look to the future and make the necessary decisions, assume the calculated risks, and invest sufficiently to keep the organization fresh, vital, and ever renewing.

From Flicker To Flame

The IATC Board of Directors has endeavored to fan the flame of Torch in meaningful and impactful ways. The board's best ideas for assuring a successful future appear in the Three-Year Strategic Plan approved in 2023. Progress has been made toward the accomplishment of the plan's measurable goals with a daunting amount of work yet to be undertaken to assure it fulfills its considerable potential. The following highlights suggest ways the board, with the full support of its constituent clubs, envisions strengthening IATC:

- *Substantially Expanded Brand Awareness:* IATC lacks the name recognition other similar organizations have achieved. Most people who would benefit from participation, and would bring life to it, have never heard of a Torch Club. The future of Torch lies in building its brand to the point that its name is recognized, and its value understood broadly. In 2023, IATC launched the Club Resource Guide and Toolkit with the intent of empowering local clubs to promote, celebrate, and expand awareness of Torch Club and its purpose. We can already see sufficient glimmers to believe a brighter future may lie ahead.

- *Enlarge and Enhance The Torch:* The magazine has won awards already, so why change it? The board believes that the magazine can play a crucial role in strengthening public awareness of Torch Club and in the generation of fresh energy within IATC. This can be accomplished by growing the magazine into a more coveted source of ideas and knowledge. It might be used to build community among Torch Club members across borders and regions. Many Torch Club presentations go unpublished because they are different from the traditional definition of what we have called a Torch Paper. By careful reexamination and expansion of what we consider publishable material, IATC may attract more submissions from local clubs, which are the magazine's lifeblood. Perhaps the magazine will stand on its own one day, reaching the level of quality that it may draw subscriptions from well beyond the active memberships of the local clubs, and even become revenue producing.

- *Develop an Awards Program to Broaden Awareness of Best Practices:* IATC must find ways to identify and award practices in use at the local level that demonstrate effectiveness in making those member organizations successful. The best practices in governance, marketing, public relations, program planning, and member recruitment and development must be surfaced, honored, and shared throughout IATC. Additionally, IATC should award not only traditional Torch Papers but other kinds of presentations that make creative use of cutting-edge technologies. We should begin giving awards to dynamic new forms of presentation.

- *Local Club and Individual Member Education:* IATC needs to provide greater benefits to each of its member organizations. IATC must play a role in providing enhanced skill development for Torch Club members. Leaders within local clubs require training in best practices in governance, marketing, public relations, program planning, and membership development. These best practices are already in use within many local clubs. As stated above, IATC can become the clearinghouse for best practices and must play a role in their dissemination so that they can be understood and implemented locally.

- **Membership Recruitment:** Age brings wisdom and perspective; youth brings energy, dynamism, and fresh ideas. Torch Club needs both age and youth. Currently the collective age of Torch Club works against the recruitment of younger members. If Torch desires to attract younger members, it must demonstrate the value it can bring to people who are in mid-career, or even at the launch of their professional lives. Understanding how best to serve younger and more diverse populations will require curiosity, inquiry, outreach, and data collection.

- **Board Excellence at the IATC Level:** We need board members recruited precisely for the expertise that is needed at this historic moment. Leaders are required in the areas of marketing, public relations, legal representation, publishing, finance, policy development and implementation, and many other realms of expertise. The IATC needs to call on the talents of very busy and highly coveted leaders in wide ranging fields if the board is to achieve the level of proficiency and skill that the future will require.

- **Economic Stability:** All organizations need adequate resources to fulfill their missions. Torch is no exception. For many years Torch has operated out of fear that dues increases would surely result in the loss of members. Healthy, growing, vital, and valuable organizations cannot operate long with a mentality of scarcity. The goal must be to build a balanced equation within which cost and value remain aligned. IATC can expect its members to pay more only if the value it delivers in return is discernable and deeply felt.

- **Staffing Requirements:** With the courage and risk tolerance that our founders possessed, we must explore options for properly staffing our organization to achieve our highest and best aspirations.

Much could be said about the recent work of the IATC Board toward implementation of new and impactful strategies. Early signs of positive change are evident because of the board's vision for the renewal of IATC. We envision *The Torch* as a magazine so refreshing to read and stimulating in content that the phone rings whenever a member's copy gets lost in the mail. We invite you to see an organization so well-resourced through growing numbers of members that it can solve its leadership problems, allowing its volunteers to invest their time and talents in the vital processes of governance and leadership. In this vision, the energy of the organization grows exponentially each year as members and clubs feel themselves served meaningfully and effectively by IATC. Imagine a future in which countless new clubs are formed because every town and city appreciates the value added by having within its boundaries a thriving Torch Club.

The challenges the IATC faces today are profound opportunities; opportunities that will enable us to build upon our first century. By lifting these rocks into their proper places and converting their weights into strengths, we will advance the noble, worthwhile vision that William Bullock proposed one hundred years ago. We will build our cathedral.

Arthur Bloom (IATC Vice President), Susan Breen-Held (IATC President)

Acknowledgments

The IATC acknowledges the contributions of the following individuals and organizations, without whom this work would not have been possible:

- ☐ The Ohio State University Archives for preserving the largest quantity of IATC records.
- ☐ Jim Coppinger, former IATC Executive Secretary, for preserving and providing minutes and other records from his term in office.
- ☐ Stephen Toy, former president, for preserving and sharing many emails, minutes and other records during his term as an officer and IATC Board member.
- ☐ Linda Porter, Anne Sterling, Ann Weller Dahl and Rich Davis for taking, preserving, and sharing many photos of past Torch events, conventions, and meetings.
- ☐ Peter Michael for his expertise as a writer and published author.
- ☐ John Vincenti for editing videos of interviews of key IATC leaders.
- ☐ Arthur E. Goldschmidt, Jr. , for tremendous record keeping and invaluable assistance accessing minutes and records from numerous decades.
- ☐ We thank Reed Taylor for his time, patience, memory, and insight during interviews touching on his service as convention manager, Regional Director, IATC President, and Editor of *The Torch.*

Supplemental Materials

Presidents of the International Association of Torch Clubs

(The names of living presidents are shown in bold.)

1924–28	F. Denton White (Minneapolis, MN)
1928–31	Burdette R. Buckingham (Columbus, OH)
1931–32	George B. Cutten (Chapel Hill, NC)
1932–34	Arthur Webster (Detroit, MI)
1934–35	George H. Ashley (Harrisburg, PA)
1935–36	William S. Linell (Portland, ME)
1936–37	W. Howard Pillsbury (Schenectady, NY)
1937–38	George B. Woods (Washington, DC)
1938–39	Lee A. White (Detroit, MI)
1939–40	Clarence E. Howell (Trenton, NJ)
1940–41	Clement G. Bowers (Binghamton, NY)
1941–42	Edgar L. Weinland (Columbus, OH)
1942–46	John C. Krantz, Jr. (Baltimore, MD)
1946–47	F.R. Murgatroyd (Hamilton, ON)
1947–48	Glenn H. Reams (Toledo, OH)
1948–49	William J. Wilcox (Allentown, PA)
1949	G.C. Carey (Buffalo, NY)
1949–51	James W. Kennedy (Cincinnati, OH)
1951–52	Leonard H. Freiberg (Cincinnati, OH)
1952–53	Elwood Street (Washington, DC)
1953–54	C.H. Stearn (Hamilton, ON)
1954–55	Marius P. Johnson (Baltimore, MD)
1955 56	W. Norris Paxton (Albany, NY)
1956–57	Karl L. Kaufman (Indianapolis, IN)
1957–58	Leonard C. Kercher (Kalamazoo, MI)
1958–59	C.A. Jones (Columbus, OH)
1959	W.H. Powe Sr. (Greenville, SC)
1959–60	Edward M. Shortt (London, ON)
1960–61	Bertram S. Nusbaum (Norfolk, VA)
1961–62	Eaton V.W. Reed (Bridgeport, CT)
1962–63	J.J. Witt (Utica, NY)
1963–64	Lon L. Nusom (San Antonio, TX)
1964–65	E. Vernon Lewis (Collegeville, PA)
1965–66	James S. Owens (Detroit, MI)
1966–67	H. Fred Heisner (Redlands, CA)
1967–68	Edgar T. Peer (St. Catharines, ON)

1968–69	Leonard M. Josephson (Knoxville, TN)
1969–70	John P. Vitko (St. Paul, MN)
1970–71	Leo M. Hauptman (Muncie, IN)
1971–72	Hilmar C. Krueger (Cincinnati, OH)
1972–73	R. Nelson Torbet (Toledo, OH)
1973–74	Norman P. Crawford (Jacksonville, FL)
1974–75	Leo G. Glasser (Wilmington, DE)
1975–76	Harry J. Krusz (Laguna Hills, CA)
1976–77	Forrest M. Smith (San Antonio, TX)
1977–78	Arthur I. Palmer, Jr. (Richmond, VA)
1978–79	Douglas M. Knudson (Wabash Valley, IN)
1979–80	Clifton E. Rogers (Harrisburg, PA)
1980–81	Fred R. Whaley, Jr. (Buffalo, NY)
1981–82	Everett H. Hopkins (Durham, NC)
1982–84	Clarence A. Peterson (Columbus, OH)
1984–86	Paul Stanfield (Des Moines, IA)
1986–88	Robert S. Rosow (San Antonio, TX)
1988–90	John M. Adams (Naples, FL)
1990–92	George P. Crepeau (Columbus, OH)
1992–94	**Richard R. Lynch** (Albany, NY)
1994	Dean C. Gross (South Hampton Roads)
1994–97	**A. Reed Taylor** (Buffalo, NY)
1997–99	Ruth Giller (Grand Rapids, MI)
1999–02	Ralph C. Falconer (Akron, OH)
2002–04	Thomas J. Bird (Chicago, IL)
2004–06	Wayne M. Davis (Loudonville, NY)
2006–08	**Anne D. Sterling** (Richmond, VA)
2008–10	**Stephen T. Toy** (Newark, DE)
2010–12	**Edward B. Latimer** (Columbia, SC)
2012–14	Charles E. Carlson (Albany, NY)
2014–16	**Norine Haas** (Frederick, MD)
2016–17	Richard Fink (Kalamazoo, MI)
2017–20	**George Conklin** (Durham, NC)
2020–2022	**Dorothy Driskell** (Columbus, OH)
2022–2024	**Susan Breen-Held** (Des Moines, IA)
2024–2026	**Art Bloom** (Winston-Salem, NC)

IATC Torch Executive Secretaries/Business Managers

Year(s)	Individuals/Businesses
1974 – 1976	Robert H. Nagel (IATC Board Member)
1976 – 1977	Thomas L. Carroll (Secretary/Treasurer)
1977 - 1980	Thomas L. Carroll (Executive Secretary)
1980 – 1995	Bostrom Management Corporation
1995 – 2009	Stickland and Jones, P.C., James V. and Gale Strickland
2010 – 2014	Association Builders
2014 – 2017	James D. Coppinger
2017 – 2020[1]	Organization Management Group (OMG)

[1] The cost of executive secretaries was becoming prohibitive and the modification of the IATC bylaws enacted in June of 2020 addressed this concern. President Conklin noted that the board might still engage professional help for some specific tasks, but that board members would now complete most of the required duties moving forward. OMG was the last management group providing an executive secretary; Outside the Cube Creative has assisted the IATC as necessary since that time.

Editors of *The Torch*

1974 to the present

Year(s)	Editor
1974-1975	W. Norris Paxton
1975-1980	Lee Hoffman
1980-1983	David Lister (also Executive Secretary)
1984	Eve Bradley[1]
1985-1991	Jeanne M. McDonald
1991-1993	Susan Moss[2]
1993-1994	Philip Lesser (also Executive Secretary; edited one issue, Winter 1994)
1994-2008[3]	R. Patrick Deans
2008-2013[3]	A. Reed Taylor
2013-2021[3]	P. Scott Stanfield
2021–Date[3]	Angela P. Dodson

[1] Eve Bradley was the first female editor of *The Torch*
[2] Susan Moss was the first person of color to edit *The Torch*.
[3] During this period, *The Torch* editors were members of Torch Clubs.

Founding and Closing of Clubs

Over its first ninety-nine years, Torch International has launched 205 clubs of which fifty remain active today, just under a 25 percent survival rate. After a slow decline in the number of clubs over many years, Torch has experienced a rebound in the 21st century, with club openings now significantly exceeding closings. IATC Club Growth 2000-2024: Thirteen new clubs were chartered.

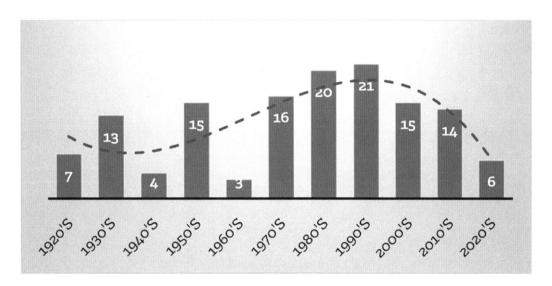

IATC Club Attrition, 1926-2024, by Decade

Current and Historical Club Locations

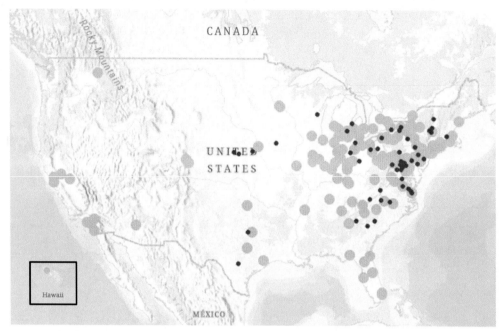

Current and Historical Club Locations (Red Dots – Active Clubs, Gray dots – Inactive Clubs)

Listing of Current and Historical Torch Clubs

Key:

- **Bold** = Currently existing clubs; Normal = Clubs no longer in existence
- Dissolved date before 2012: A club was not listed in 2012-13 *Red Book.*
- Dissolved date after 2013: A club was listed in 2012-13 *Red Book* but no longer exists.
- The survival census is a countdown from the 205 clubs that have ever existed to the 50 operating as of the time of publication of *Sharing the Light.* It is not a timeline.

Club #	Name	Charter	Dissolved Date
1a	Minneapolis, MN	7/10/1924	9/3/2003
1b	St.Paul, MN	1924-1925	1926
1c	Dallas, TX	1924-1925	1926
1d	Oklahoma OK	1924-1925	1926
2	**Fort Worth, TX**	**4/16/1925**	**Active**
3	**Rochester, NY**	**3/15/1926**	**Active**
4	Utica, NY	5/3/1926	Between 1986 - 96
5	Syracuse, NY	5/10/1926	3/14/1997
6	**Albany, NY**	**6/30/1926**	**Active**
7	**Buffalo, NY**	**7/1/1926**	**Active**
8	**Akron, OH**	**11/8/1926**	**Active**
9	Canton, OH	12/13/1926	Before 1979
10	**Columbus, OH**	**12/16/1926**	**Active**
11	Dayton, OH	1/24/1927	1931
12	Louisville, KY	3/14/1927	1930
13	Cincinnati, OH	3/28/1927	7/15/19
14	Indianapolis, IN	5/23/1927	1992
15	Erie, PA	11/21/1927	1929
16	**Toledo, OH**	**12/12/1927**	**Active**
17	Cleveland, OH	12/15/1927	1940
18	York, PA	1/5/1928	Between 1981-86
19	**Youngstown, OH**	**1/5/1928**	**Active**
20	Lansing, MI	2/15/1928	1930
21	Pittsburgh, PA	4/13/1928	1930
22	Johnstown, PA	4/24/1928	1929
23	Altoona, PA	4/24/1928	1930
24	Grand Rapids, MI	5/15/28	2016
25	Detroit, MI/Windsor, ON,Canada	6/21/1928	5/12/04

Club #	Name	Charter	Dissolved Date
26	Reading, PA	7/6/28	Between 2015-20
27	Flint, MI	7/6/1928	1930
28	**Saginaw Valley, MI**	**8/7/28**	**Active**
29	Springfield, OH	11/20/1928	1933
30	Washington, DC	12/11/1928	7/21/05
31	Jackson, MI	2/19/1929	1936
32	Kalamazoo, MI	3/21/1929	6/1/19
33	Battle Creek, MI	4/12/1929	1929
34	Lima, OH	5/9/1929	1923
35	Harrisburg, PA	5/13/1929	5/10/11
36	Portland, Western Maine	9/30/1929	2016
37	Niagara, ONT, CA	11/7/29	1934
38	Binghamton, NY	12/9/1929	1971
39	**Lehigh Valley, PA (Allentown)**	**1/8/1930**	**Active**
40	Essex County, NJ	3/3/1930	1986
41	Scranton, PA	2/24/1930	1935
42	**Trenton, NJ**	**4/14/1930**	**Active**
43	**Elmira, NY**	**5/15/1930**	**Active**
44	**Delaware (Wilmington)**	**6/16/1930**	**Active**
45	Hartford, CT	11/5/1930	1933
46	**Schenectady, NY**	**1/20/1931**	**Active**
47	Baltimore, MD	3/19/1931	2015
48	Richmond, VA	4/28/1931	1936
49	Troy, NY	11/3/1932	1940
50	**Lancaster, PA (Millersville)**	**5/1/1933**	**Active**
51	Paterson, NJ	6/27/1933	1936
52	Oakland County, MI	4/9/1935	Before 1976
53	Fingers Lake, NY	4/23/1936	Between 1986-96
54	St. Lawrence County, NY	4/27/1936	1972
55	Auburn, NY	11/13/1936	Between 1981-86
56	Oswego-Fulton, NY	4/19/1937	1971
57	Battle Creek, MI	11/15/1937	1950
58	Muskegon, MI	4/29/1938	2020
59	Hamilton, ONT, CA	4/11/1939	Between 1976-79
60	South Hampton Roads (Norfolk, Va)	1/26/1939	2/4/21
61	Raleigh, NC	3/30/1939	3/14/97
62	Atlanta, GA	4/10/1939	1948
63	Central Florida, FL	4/11/1939	1945

Club #	Name	Charter	Dissolved Date
64	**Winston-Salem, NC**	**12/14/1939**	**Active**
65	Cumberland Valley, PA	1/29/1940	5/31/02
66	**Worcester, MA**	**3/1/1940**	**Active**
67	**Wyoming Valley, PA (Dallas)**	**3/13/1940**	**Active**
68	Boston, MA	5/23/1940	1957
69	Niagara, NY	6/10/1940	1972
70	Knoxville, TN	7/17/1940	2014
71	Philadelphia, PA	3/17/1941	1957
72	Western South Carolina (Greenville)	3/25/1941	2020
73	**Richmond, VA**	**4/14/1941**	**Active**
74	Olean, NY	2/9/1942	1967
75	Jacksonville, FL	4/13/1942	Between 1981-86
76	Morgantown, WV	11/20/1942	1953
77	Houston, TX	4/10/1944	5/29/08
78	Lexington, KY	1945	Between 1981-86
79	Northern Chautauqua, NY	5/26/1947	7/23/03
80	Louisville, KY.	5/28/1947	1959
81	San Francisco, CA	6/26/1947	1952
82	**Durham-Chapel Hill, NC**	**9/17/1947**	**Active**
83	Jamestown, NY	12/12/1947	3/26/03
84	**Erie, PA**	**2/25/1948**	**Active**
85	Memphis, TN	4/19/1948	1952
86	Bridgeport, CT	4/27/1948	1973
87	Cleveland, OH	5/25/1948	1951
88	Nashville, TN	5/12/1949	5/10/11
89	Chattanooga, TN	5/13/1949	1992
90	**Columbia, SC**	**11/15/1949**	**Active**
91	Wabash Valley, IN	1/10/1950	1992
92	Indianapolis, IN	1/11/1950	1992
93	Terre Haute, IN	3/13/1950	Before 1976
94	Fort Wayne, IN	3/27/1950	Before 1976
95	Muncie, IN	3/29/1950	9/24/01
96	Manhattan, NY	4/18/1950	1952
97	Bloomington, IN	2/20/1951	1959
98	Butler County, OH	12/13/1950	10/31/12
99	Bloomington, IL	2/20/1951	1959
100	Champaign County, IL	2/21/1951	10/25/04
101	Windsor, ONT, CA	9/27/1951	6/1/86

Club #	Name	Charter	Dissolved Date
102	Allegany County, NY	10/23/1951	Between 1976-79
103	Providence, RI	1/31/1952	1953
104	**Gettysburg-Adams County, PA**	**3/25/52**	**Active**
105	**Hagerstown, MD**	**5/1/52**	**Active**
106	Roanoke Valley, VA (Rockingham)	1/6/53	6/1/81
107	York, PA	1/12/1953	6/1/81
108	Frederick, MD	1/22/1953	1958
109	Greensboro, NC	1/29/1953	Before 1976
110	Carlisle, PA	2/23/1953	1954
111	Tallahassee, Fl	3/16/1953	1991
112	London, ONT, CA	3/23/1954	Before 1976
113	**San Antonio, TX**	**5/10/54**	**Active**
114	Sonoma County, CA	9/30/54	1978
115	Ithaca, NY	3/10/55	4/1/83
116	Port Huron, MI	3/23/55	1974
117	Bradford,PA	5/20/59	1960
118	Firelands-Sandusky, OH	3/29/55	10/30/12
119	**Central PA (State College), PA**	**4/13/55**	**Active**
120	Pittsburgh, PA	5/24/55	Before 1976
121	Sarnia, ONT, CA	9/30/55	1956
122	Columbia-Montour, PA	11/21/55	1/24/2019
123	**Des Moines (Central Iowa), IA**	**12/14/55**	**Active**
124	Dayton, OH	1/24/56	5/1/1997
125	Connecticut Valley, CT	6/3/57	1972
126	Denver, CO	1/14/59	1973
127	St. Paul, MN	3/19/59	Between 1986-96
128	Bradford,PA	5/20/1959	1960
129	**Lansing, MI**	**10/14/59**	**Active**
130	Stanislaus County, CA	2/11/60	1974
131	San Bernadino, CA	3/9/60	Before 1976
132	Minneapolis, MN	4/20/60	9/3/03
133	Boulder, CO	4/21/60	2018
134	Sacramento, CA	5/17/1960	8/19/02
135	Pikes Pike, CO	6/21/1960	Between 1986-96
136	La Jolla, CA	10/6/1960	Between 1981-86
137	**St. Catharines, ONT, CA**	**11/23/1960**	**Active**
138	**Hampton Roads, VA (Virginia Beach)**	**4/6/1961**	**Active**
139	Scottsdale-On-The-Desert, AZ	5/23/1961	Between 1981-86

Club #	Name	Charter	Dissolved Date
140	Washington Square, NY	1/18/1962	1973
141	**Portsmouth, VA**	**4/25/1962**	**Active**
142	Charlottesville, VA	5/2/1962	3/18/1998
143	Chicago, IL	5/22/1962	2014
144	Long Island, NY	5/23/1962	1963
145	Cleveland, OH	4/1/1981	3/13/12
146	**Lincoln, NE**	**5/20/1963**	**Active**
147	Toronto, Ont, CA	1/22/1965	Between 1976-79
148	Long Beach, CA	3/16/1965	Between 1986-96
149	**Athens, GA**	**5/13/1965**	**Active**
150	Richmond, KY	1/25/1966	Between 1981-86
151	Grand Valley, ONT, CA	1/26/1966	Between 1976-79
152	**Montgomery County, VA**	**2/23/1967**	**Active**
153	Fort Lauderdale, FL	3/20/1967	1974
154	Delaware County, PA	10/16/1967	Between 1981-86
155	Charlotte, NC	1/25/1968	1974
156	Gainesville, FL	4/15/1968	7/18/1997
157	**Augusta, GA**	**11/6/1968**	**Active**
158	Decatur, IL	6/12/1969	1972
159	Boca Raton, Fl	4/14/1975	7/4/08
160	Greater Orlando, FL	4/21/1971	Between 1976-79
161	Honolulu, HI	6/14/1971	Between 1981-1986
162	Central, TX (Temple, TX)	3/27/1973	10/25/1999
163	Wheeling, WV	5/22/1974	Between 1986-96
164	Laguna Hills, CA	5/27/1974	1984
165	Stroudsburg Area, PA	6/10/1975	8/31/21
166	Pinellas, FL (Tampa)	6/17/1975	6/1/81
170	Michiana (Notre Dame + South Bend)	6/1/1976	1979
171	Finlay, OH	5/9/1979	Between 1986-96
172	**Winchester, VA**	**3/5/1980**	**Active**
173	Omaha, NB	5/1/1981	Before 1976
174	Greater Rochester Area, MN	9/1/1975	10/26/2019
175	Bucks County, PA	6/1/1994	Between 2003-06
176	Heartland, FL	6/2/1995	3/13/2000
177	Rockford IL	6/13/1995	1996
178	**Frederick, MD**	**6/20/1995**	**Active**
179	James Rumsey, WV	3/12/1998	2015
185	**Fox Valley-Appleton WI**	**4/15/1999**	**Active**

Club #	Name	Charter	Dissolved Date
186	Waynesboro Area, PA	5/4/2000	9/4/08
187	**Geneseo, NY**	**4/19/2001**	**Active**
188	**Adirondack, NY (Ticonderoga)**	**5/2/2002**	**Active**
189	**Tristate Regional, Cumberland, MD**	**5/13/2023**	**Active**
190	Asheville-Blue Ridge, NC	4/6/2005	2015
191	Chambersburg, MD	4/11/2005	2024
192	Shenandoah Valley, Martinsburg, WV	4/3/2007	2009
193	**Blue Ridge, Leesburg, VA**	**5/8/2007**	**Active**
194	**High Country, (Boone) NC**	**5/12/2008**	**Active**
195	**Westminster, MD**	**6/1/2010**	**Active**
196	**Kearney, NE**	**3/12/2012**	**Active**
197	**Hastings, NE**	**11/15/2012**	**Active**
198	South East NB	9/9/2013	2021
199	**Fredericksburg, VA**	**11/18/2015**	**Active**
200	**Saratoga, NY**	**4/7/2016**	**Active**
201	Wayne, NB	9/1/2016	before 2022
202	**Williamsburg, VA**	**6/22/2023**	**Active**

Torch Membership Trends 1974-2024

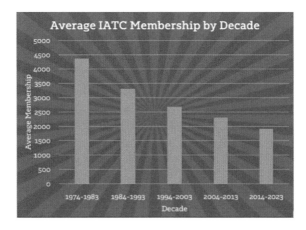

The average number of Torch members by decade

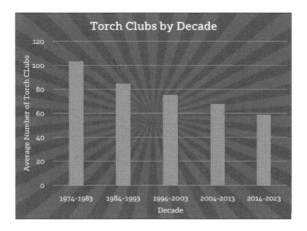

The number of Torch Clubs by decade

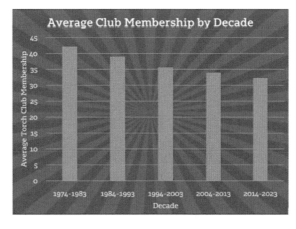

The average club membership by decade

Annual Torch Convention Host Cities

1927	Buffalo, NY	1956	Albany & Schenectady, NY
1928	Columbus, OH	1957	Fort Monroe & Norfolk, VA
1929	Cincinnati, OH	1958	Detroit, MI
1930	No convention	1959	Greenville, SC
1931	Washington, DC	1960	Indianapolis, IN
1932	Albany, NY	1961	Hartford, CT
1933	No convention Depression	1962	Toledo, OH
1934	Detroit, MI	1963	Utica, NY
1935	Utica, NY	1964	Knoxville, TN
1936	Harrisburg, PA	1965	Buffalo, NY
1937	Rochester, NY	1966	Cincinnati, OH
1938	Toledo, OH	1967	Grand Rapids, MI
1939	Binghamton, NY	1968	Washington, DC
1940	Portland, ME	1969	Durham, NC
1941	Baltimore, MD	1970	Windsor, ON, CA
1942	Grand Rapids, MI	1971	Nashville, TN
1943	No convention WW II	1972	Sebasco, ME
1944	No convention WW II	1973	San Antonio, TX
1945	No convention WW II	1974	St. Paul, MN
1946	Wilmington, DE	1975	Orlando, FL
1947	Hamilton, ON, CA	1976	Columbus, OH
1948	Reading, PA	1977	Long Beach & Laguna Hills, CA
1949	Richmond, VA	1978	Harrisburg, PA
1950	Lexington, KY	1979	Norfolk, VA
1951	Rochester, NY	1980	Kalamazoo, MI
1952	Columbus, OH	1981	Washington, DC
1953	Trenton, NJ	1982	Knoxville, TN
1954	Cincinnati, OH	1983	Albany & Schenectady, NY
1955	Baltimore, MD	1984	Toledo, OH

1985	Des Moines, IA	2016	Columbus, OH
1986	Richmond, VA	2017	Kalamazoo, MI
1987	Akron, OH	2018	San Antonio, TX
1988	Bay City & Saginaw, MI	2019	Durham, NC
1989	San Antonio, Texas	2020	No convention COVID
1990	Lehigh Valley & Bethlehem, PA	2021	No convention COVID
1991	Buffalo, NY	2022	Saratoga, NY
1992	Columbus, OH	2023	Baltimore, MD (5 nearby clubs)
1993	Portland, ME	2024	Richmond, VA
1994	Norfolk, VA		
1995	Detroit, MI		
1996	Albany, NY		
1997	Wilmington, DE		
1998	Kalamazoo, MI		
1999	Toledo, OH		
2000	Winchester, VI		
2001	St. Catharine's, ON, CA		
2002	Athens, GA		
2003	Chicago, IL		
2004	Wyoming Valley, Wilkes Barre, PA		
2005	Des Moines, IA		
2006	Lehigh Valley & Bethlehem, PA		
2007	Richmond, VA		
2008	Lancaster, PA		
2009	Fox Valley & Appleton, WI		
2010	Youngstown, OH		
2011	Hagerstown, MD		
2012	Portsmouth & Norfolk, VA		
2013	Columbia, SC		
2014	St. Catharine's, ON, CA		
2015	Lincoln, NE		

Paxton Award Laureate

1976	W. Norris Paxton
1977	Seymour A. Horwitz
1978	James E. Ingram
1979	Jack E. Gieck
1980	John W. Allen
1981	John F. Brown
1982	Robert E. Shepherd, Jr.
1983	Harry D. Lewis
1984	Dan Pletta
1985	Jerry L. Petr
1986	John H. D. Bryan
1987	E. Cabell Brand
1988	Hubert J. Davis
1989	Warner M. Montgomery
1990	Jesse R. Long
1991	Earnest R. Oney
1992	Kathryn P. Clausen
1993	Charles G. Beaudette
1994	Thomas L. Minnick
1995	C. Walter Clark
1996	Richard Schellhase
1997	Leanne Wade Beorn
1998	Gerald G. Eggert
1999	Mary Frances Forcier
2000	Robert G. Neuhauser
2001	Jonathan B. Wight
2002	Richard T. Schellhase
2003	Mark Lore
2004	Matthew T. Taylor, Sr.

2005	Robert G. Neuhauser
2006	Malcolm M. Marsden
2007	Edward P. Blazer
2008	Arthur B. Gunlicks
2009	Charles W. Darling
2010	Barton C. Shaw
2011	Danny J. Krebs
2012	Roland F. Moy
2013	Leland W. Robinson
2014	Henry Ticknor
2015	Roger Hughes
2016	John P. Lewis
2017	Stephen Sterrett
2018	Roland F. Moy
2019	Leland W. Robinson
2020	Eric J. Davis
2021	Judah Ginsberg
2022	Lowell Satre
2023	P. Scott Stanfield

Gold Award Recipients

1987   Thomas Carroll, Lincoln, NE, Robert L. Stern, Norfolk, VA

1988   Robert Rosow, San Antonio, TX

1989   Arthur I. Palmer, Jr., Richmond, VA, Dr. Edgar Peer, St.Catharines, ON, CA

1990   Everett Hopkins, Durham-Chapel, NC

1991   Clarence Peterson, Columbus, OH

1992   Dr. Leo M. Hauptman, Muncie, IN, Chauncey M. Depuy, Cumberland Valley, PA

1993   Hubert J. Davis, Portsmouth, VA, Paul Stanfield, Des Moines, IA,
        Fred R. Whaley, Jr., Buffalo, NY, John Adams, Lehigh Valley, PA

1994   Alice Rohr, Schenectady, NY

1995   Dean Gross, Norfolk, VA

1996   Dr. George P. Crepeau, Columbus, OH, Richard R. Lynch, Albany, NY

1997   A. Reed Taylor, Buffalo, NY, Bruce C. Souders, Winchester, VA

1998   No Gold Awards

1999   Mary Alice Butkofsky, Lancaster, PA, John A. Mapp, Richmond, VA

2000   R. Patrick Deans, South Hampton Roads, VA, Ruth E. Giller, Grand Rapids, MI,
        Edward B. Latimer, Columbia, SC

2001   David Craig, St. Catharines, ON, CA, Leo Kellogg, Albany, NY
        Norman H. Wright, Rochester, NY

2002   Ralph C. Falconer, Akron, OH

2003   Charles Greeb, Jr., Winchester, VA, Allan R. Powell, Hagerstown, MD,
        William S. Troxell, Richmond, VA

2004   Gilles O. Allard, Athens, GA, William E. Elstran (Posthumous), Durham-Chapel Hill, NC

2005   Thomas J. Bird, Chicago, IL, David C. Smith, Western Maine, ME,
        Stephen T. Toy, Delaware, DE

2006	Charles E. Carlson, Albany, NY, Catherine Fleisher, Elmira, NY
2007	H. Jeremy Packard, Wyoming Valley, PA
2008	Ann Weller Dahl, Baltimore, MD, George B. DuBois, Jr., Frederick, MD
2009	John A. Horner, Jr., Cleveland, OH, Meredith Rousseau, Lancaster, PA
2010	Anne Sterling, Richmond, VA, Leonard W. Weiss, Fox Valley, WI
2011	Linda Porter, Youngstown, OH, Rev. Theodore (Ted) Haas, Frederick, MD, Ivan Hrabowsky, St.Catharines, ON, CA
2012	Dr. Joseph Vincent, Lehigh Valley, PA, Edith Reynolds White, South Hampton Roads,VA
2013	No Gold Awards
2014	Linda D. Jefferson, Columbus, OH, Francis D. Moul, Lincoln, NE
2015	No Gold Awards
2016	George Conklin, Durham-Chapel Hill, NC, George Heron, Saginaw Valley, MI
2017	Norine Haas, Frederick, MD
2018	Dorothy Driskell, Columbus, OH
2019	Paul Scott Stanfield, Lincoln, NE
2020	Roger Kramer, San Antonio, TX
2021	Richard Davis, Columbus, OH
2022	Elizabeth Short, Columbus, OH
2023	Lynn Bernard, Fredericksburg, VA, Dwight Williams, Midland, MI

Torch Foundation Presidents

Forrest M. Smith, Jr., 1979 (incorporation year) to 1987

Clarence Peterson, 1987-1993

George Crepeau, 1994-2004

Ralph Falconer, 2004-2009

Walter van Eck, 2009-2012

Anne Sterling, 2012-2014

Richard R. Lynch, 2014-2017

Anne Sterling, 2017-2019

Sue Breen-Held, 2019-2021

Richard R. Lynch, June-September, 2021

Pat Shutterly, September 2021-current

The Writing Team

Arthur L. Bloom

Art has had a diverse career as an investment counselor, municipal bond trader, bank advertising manager, and retail furniture business owner. In 2000, he founded The Bloom Agency, an award-winning marketing, advertising, and PR firm that was cited as one of the fastest-growing companies in Piedmont Triad, NC. After selling the agency, Art became a certified business coach. Art has served in board leadership roles for Arbor Acres Retirement Community, UNC School of the Arts Foundation, Piedmont Opera, Senior Services, Winston Salem Youth Chorus, Piedmont Wind Symphony, and Interfaith Winston Salem. He served for twenty-five years as cantorial soloist for Temple Emanuel and conducts a seventy person show choir at Arbor Acres. In 2023, Art was awarded the National United Methodist Association Mission Award for harnessing the power of music to engage, inspire, and connect with others. While serving as IATC President, Art will also serve as Chair of the Piedmont Triad Juvenile Diabetes Research Foundation (JDRF) Board.

Ann Weller Dahl

Ann Weller Dahl is a "legacy" member of the IATC, having joined the Baltimore Torch Club in 1990, following in her father's footsteps. For three years she served as the Director of Region 3. In 2008 she received IATC's Gold Award at the Lancaster Convention. Since the Torch Foundation was reorganized in 2008-09, Ann has twice served as a trustee and for six years was the secretary. Ann is now a member of the Westminster, Maryland, Torch Club. She has attended many IATC conventions and was very involved in planning the 2023 Convention in Baltimore. Currently she is forming a new Torch Club in Towson, Maryland. After graduating from Goucher College and obtaining a Master's Degree in Education from Johns Hopkins University, Ann taught for three decades at the Calvert School and wrote curricula for the school's home schooling division.

Arthur Goldschmidt

Arthur Goldschmidt was born in Washington, DC, and educated at Georgetown Day School, Friends Seminary in New York, Colby College in Waterville, Maine, the American University of Beirut, and Harvard University. He taught Middle East history and related subjects at Penn State from 1965 to 2000. He is the author of *A Concise History of the Middle East* (now in its thirteenth edition), *A Brief History of Egypt, A Biographical Dictionary of Modern Egypt,* and *Historical Dictionary of Egypt* (now in its fifth edition). He also received numerous awards for teaching and advising, as well as the Middle East Studies Association's Mentoring Award in 2000. He joined the Torch Club of Central Pennsylvania in 1986, served as its president in 1993, and since 2011 as its secretary. He chaired the IATC's History Committee (2004-2017) and joined the Centennial History Project in 2021.

Richard R. Lynch

Richard R. "Dick" Lynch grew up in southeastern Massachusetts. He graduated from Providence College with an undergraduate major in Economics and a minor in Philosophy in 1964. He worked in the New York State governor's budget division for fifteen years. After acquiring a master's degree in public administration with a major in public finance from Rockefeller College, State University of New York, Albany, he spent the last seventeen years of his career as chief financial officer of the State Department of Environmental Conservation. Dick joined the Albany Torch Club in 1977 and soon took leadership positions. He became a regional director and was president of the IATC from 1992 to 1994. He was a charter member of the Saratoga, New York, Club, and a Founders Society member of the IATC's Centennial Club. Dick is a Lifetime Member of the Torch Foundation who has served as its secretary/treasurer and president. He is currently a trustee of the Torch Foundation.

Douglas Punger

Doug Punger was raised on Long Island, New York. He attended Wake Forest University majoring in History and Political Science and graduating from its School of Law. Doug served as General Counsel for the Winston-Salem/Forsyth County Schools for about thirty-three years and was in private practice for another ten. He taught as an adjunct professor of Education Law at Wake Forest. He has presented papers on education law at national, regional, and state conferences. He has served on and chaired a number of non-profit community organizations and boards. Doug joined the Torch Club of Winston-Salem, North Carolina, in 2008. He served as club secretary for three terms, vice president, and president. Doug has made three presentations to the club. One was on the history of the Winston-Salem Torch Club, which caught the attention of Leo Kellogg and others who invited him serve on and then co-chair the IATC Centennial History Project.

Paul Scott Stanfield

Scott Stanfield is the son of onetime IATC President Paul Stanfield and his wife Salee, both of whom were Torch Club members. Educated at Grinnell College and Northwestern University, he is the author of *Yeats and Politics in the 1930s* and various articles on Yeats and other modernist writers. He taught in the English Department of Nebraska Wesleyan University for thirty-four years and has been a Torch member even longer than that, having joined the Lincoln, Nebraska, Club in 1986. He edited *The Torch* from 2013 to 2021. In 2023 he received the 2023 Paxton Award for his paper "Stay in Your Lane: Who Gets to Tell the Stories of a Culture?"

Liz Teufel

Liz Teufel earned a Bachelor's Degree in Interior Design and Related Art and a Master's Degree in Teaching from the University of Iowa. Upon graduation she began a forty-five year career teaching for the Des Moines Public Schools, at first doing home economics outreach work with disadvantaged people, then helping to create and teach in a child abuse prevention program, and in later years teaching Family and Consumer Science in an inner-city classroom. Upon retirement she returned to the classroom as a substitute teacher, but this phase of her career was ended by the COVID epidemic. Liz was a member and eventually president of the Des Moines Child Abuse Prevention Council. She joined the Des Moines Women's Club, serving on many committees and becoming its president. She served on the Hoyt Sherman Place Foundation Board and chaired its Art and Artifacts Committee. She has recently joined the Central Iowa Torch Club.

Evan Thomas

Evan Thomas earned a Bachelor's Degree in Education from Chicago State University and an M.A. and Ph.D. in History from the University of Iowa. Before retirement from Grand View University in Des Moines he taught Western Civilization and other courses, including Modern Japan, Modern Russia, Contemporary US History, and History of Women in Professions. He co-edited a book of essays, *The Grand View Reader*, and contributed the chapter "Eleven Decades of Student Life." He is the co-author of two textbooks: *America since 1900*, and *Moving On: The American People since 1945*. He has made several presentations to his local Torch Club, including "Ourselves to Know: Exploring Human Prehistory." Another presentation, "Thomas Midgely, Jr, and the Fate of the Earth" was published in the Spring 2023 issue of *The Torch*. Evan is President of the Central Iowa Torch Club.

John Tordiff

John joined the St. Catharines Torch Club in 2006. After serving as treasurer, bulletin editor, and vice president, he became Club President in 2009-2010 and again in 2023-2024. He was employed in the retail industry for over thirty years while simultaneously helping found and/or serving on the board of several local community groups. He has degrees in Political Science and Education from Brock University as well as a Master's Degree in Political Science from the University of Guelph. He has interviewed a past Prime Minister, provincial and federal cabinet ministers, and senior government environmental officials. He has written academic papers on the Great Lakes Water Quality Agreement and on Government Secrecy and Departmental Discretion. He has traveled extensively including cruises covering both the North Atlantic (stopping in Iceland) and the North Pacific (with a stop in Siberia).

Joseph L. Zawicki

A science teacher at heart, Joe was born and raised in Western New York, the son of Leo and Rita Zawicki. He was intrigued by math and science in high school and went on to earn a Bachelor's Degree in Biology, a Master's Degree in Education, and a doctorate that focused on the study of alternative performance assessment formats in physics. He taught high school science for thirteen years, and has been at Buffalo State University since 2001, teaching science courses and working with pre- and in-service science teachers. He joined the Buffalo Torch Club in 2011 and has since become the director of IATC Region 10. He is currently the president of the Western New York STEM Hub, and co-president of the New York STEM Education Collaborative. While teaching full time, Joe has had primary responsibility for formatting *Sharing the Light*.

The Researching Team

Chris Atzberger

Christina Atzberger holds a Master of Science in Library Science degree. She retired from Adult Services and Reference services from a public library, and as a professional genealogist. She is a member of the Columbus Torch Club.

Rich Davis

Rich Davis was on the faculty of and in leadership roles for the Medical Center at The Ohio State University. He is a member and Past President of The Columbus Torch Club.

Raimund Goerler

Professor Raimund Goerler retired from The Ohio State University, where he was University Archivist and Assistant Director of Libraries. Rai has been president of the Columbus Torch Club.

Diane Selby

Paul Scott Stanfield

Scott Stanfield was an invaluable member of both the writing and the researching teams. His full statement appears under the writing team heading in the previous section.

Stephen Toy

John R. Vincenti

John R. Vincenti was past chapter president and webmaster for the State College, PA, IATC.

Nancy Wardwell

Nancy Wardwell is retired faculty from The Ohio State University, past President of the Columbus Torch Club, and Region 5 Director on the IATC Board.

Made in the USA
Columbia, SC
11 June 2024

4cdda133-402c-4448-956e-2dbe626d6a28R01